JOYOUS MACHINES:
MICHAEL LANDY AND JEAN TINGUELY

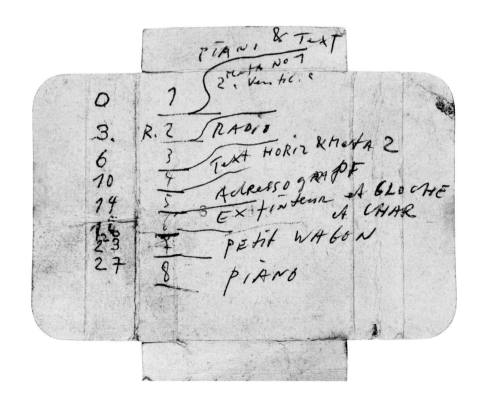

Michael
Landy,
H2NY
My Head
on His
Shoulders
2007

JOYOUS MACHINES:
MICHAEL LANDY AND JEAN TINGUELY

Edited by Laurence Sillars

Contents

6   Foreword

9   Failing to Fail: Michael Landy and Jean Tinguely
Laurence Sillars

39   Log, March 17, 1960
Dore Ashton

131   Heavy Meta: Landy and Tinguely in the Dump
Michael Landy

138   List of Exhibited Works

142   Sponsors and Donors

144   Photocredits

Foreword

In 1982 the Tate Gallery in London, now Tate Britain, presented a retrospective exhibition of the Swiss sculptor Jean Tinguely. One of the most radical, witty and inventive artists of his time, Tinguely perhaps more than any other artist was responsible for bringing physical movement to art, rather than its mere allusion. Using the most basic of materials, more often than not found in the junk yard, his sculptures made poignant social comment, examined the ever changing relationship between humankind and the machine, and at the same time sent established notions of modernist art history spinning – quite literally.

The Tate Gallery exhibition brought Tinguely's work to the attention of audiences in the UK on an expansive scale for the time. It also introduced his work to a young Michael Landy, then still a student, who has gone on to become one of the most respected and admired artists at work in Britain today. *Joyous Machines: Michael Landy and Jean Tinguely* is an exhibition that celebrates Tinguely's influence upon him. Co-curated by Michael, with Laurence Sillars, Curator at Tate Liverpool, it brings a unique perspective to Tinguely's lesser-known early works, tracing a path from his beginnings as an artist through to the spectacular auto-destructive sculpture-happening *Homage to New York*, 1960. This, now mythical, event has preoccupied Michael for many years in his numerous drawings and a new documentary film, shown here for the very first time courtesy of The Channel 4 BRITDOC Foundation. It is Michael's long standing desire to recreate the event as the ultimate 'homage' to his hero.

First and foremost, we would like to thank Michael for his generosity, wisdom, humour and tireless enthusiasm for this project. It has been both a privilege and a pleasure to work with him. The exhibition would simply not have been possible without the support of the Museum Jean Tinguely, Basel and we would, especially, like to thank Roland Wetzel, Director, Andres Pardey, Deputy Director, along with Laurentia Leon and Claire Wueest. We are also indebted to Guido Magnaguagno, the previous director of the Tinguely Museum who enthusiastically supported this project from the outset. Their advice, time, energy and ready agreement to a substantial number of loans has been invaluable.

We would also like to express our sincere gratitude to Bloum Cardenas, representative of the Tinguely Estate for her generous support of this project. It was a pleasure to work with her again following the successful Niki de Saint Phalle exhibition at Tate Liverpool last year. Pro Helvetia, the Swiss Arts Council, have provided generous financial support allowing us to realise this ambitious endeavour, as have Paul and Margrit Hahnloser-Ingold. We would further like to thank all of the lenders to the exhibition who have so generously agreed to part with much valued works for the duration of the show. We are indebted to them all. Thomas Dane and Leigh Robb of Thomas Dane Gallery, London, and Carolyn Alexander of Alexander and Bonin, New York, have also been constant sources of support and advice. Finally, we would also like to thank Michel Dutilleul-Francoeur, Paris for his help and guidance.

At Tate we would like to thank Laurence Sillars who curated the exhibition, in close collaboration with Michael, and edited this publication, applying his customary intelligence and sensitivity to create an important and beautiful presentation. We are also grateful to Darren Pih, Assistant Curator, whose thoughtfulness, calm and expertise have been felt in so many areas of the exhibition's preparation. We are most grateful to Wendy Lothian, Ken Simons, Barry Bentley and Roger Sinek for their care and professionalism in organising the complex tasks of shipping and installation, along with our team of conservators, Jo Gracey, Franziska Herzog and Rachel Scott. Ian Malone provided invaluable assistance producing this publication and Herman Lelie and Stefania Bonelli, as ever, have come up with a wonderfully fitting design. Our sincere gratitude also goes to Dore Ashton who has so kindly allowed us to reproduce her wonderful account of the day of *Homage to New York*, 17 March 1960.

In his foreword to the 1982 exhibition, Alan Bowness wrote that a Tinguely exhibition is 'never an altogether predictable occasion... though always a noisy one!' This exhibition, although not without its sonic accompaniments, presents a subtler side to Tinguely's work, alongside Michael's many responses to *Homage to New York*. We are delighted to have the opportunity to present their 'joyous machines'.

Christoph Grunenberg
Director

Andrea Nixon
Executive Director

Failing to Fail: Michael Landy and Jean Tinguely

Laurence Sillars

The machine is an instrument that permits me to be poetic. If you respect the machine, if you enter into a game with the machine, then perhaps you can make a truly joyous machine – by joyous I mean free. [1]

1
Jean Tinguely in Calvin Tomkins, *Ahead of the Game*, Harmondsworth, Penguin, 1968, p.140.

2
Quotations unless stated otherwise are from conversations with the artist.

In 1982, then a textiles student at Loughborough, Michael Landy visited the Tate Gallery's Jean Tinguely retrospective. Given what we know of his work today, textiles was not the obvious choice. His enthusiasm for systems – 'I was an obsessive pattern-maker with a dislike of fabric' – has been mapped onto some of his most significant works to date, the numerous cut-out figures of *Scrapheap Services* for example. Yet beyond that, the embroidery class was perhaps not the burgeoning creative environment he had craved: 'the most exciting bit was when the needle from a sewing machine embedded itself in a girl's finger and I got to pull it out.'[2] Knowing little of the artist before his visit, Landy's swift and immersive induction to the world of Tinguely, confronted by dozens of weird and wonderful machines, a cacophony of bangs, crashes, whirrings, smashes and stray musical notes, was a revelation. To an extent, traces of Tinguely's influence have been identifiable in Landy's work ever since – a shared appropriation of waste materials, the use of consumer culture and its systems to make wider social comment – and in 2006 he began an extensive series of drawings made directly after him. Whether explicit in his work or not, however, Landy's enthusiasm for Tinguely continues with great fervour and it was the starting point for this exhibition: Michael Landy's 'homage' to Jean Tinguely.

Tinguely (1925–91) was one of the most radical and subversive sculptors of the 20th Century whose work was typified by its irony, parody,

fig.1
Jean Tinguely
Composition, 1947
41 x 56 cm

10

3
Hultén, *Jean Tinguely: Méta*, London, Thames and Hudson, 1975, p.7.

4
Ibid., p.8.

humour and inventiveness. Using junk as his basic material, he was seldom happier than when plundering a scrap heap, hunting out the newly discarded. On a visit to a New York tip he once remarked that he could, after finding the right girl, quite easily live there. Born in Fribourg, Switzerland, he studied at the Basel School of Arts and Crafts in the early 1940s, albeit sporadically through irregular attendance. He acquired a thorough understanding of the history of modern art, learning of De Stijl, Bauhaus, Wassily Kandinsky, the Surrealists and began also to hear of the work of Vladimir Tatlin, Kasimir Malevich and Alexander Calder.[3] All were to become important influences, and Tinguely's enthusiasm for both historical and contemporary artistic developments in Europe and North America was apparent in his work throughout this career.

Tinguely's earliest works – dense, angular, geometric abstract paintings – were unsurprising given the dominance of such painting in contemporary Europe (fig.1). Their latent sense of movement, however, was an indication of the direction he would soon take. Motion in art was a preoccupation long held by the artists Tinguely had studied and was following, from the Futurists in Italy to Jackson Pollock in the United States. But physically setting objects into motion was a quality seldom previously achieved, Naum Gabo being a notable exception and precedent. As Pontus Hultén, critic, curator, friend, and promoter of Tinguely's noted, 'the idea of setting pictorial forms in motion undoubtedly existed in the minds of a large number of artists, and jokes were probably made about it in many artists' studios. It is typical of Tinguely's attitude to art that in this situation he set out to realise what plenty of others had thought of but had not carried out.'[4]

As part of his incessant experimentation and engineering, Tinguely had studied the visual and physical impact different kinds of movement had upon objects. Even as a teenager, without any claims to making 'art', he would retreat into the forest to make intricate systems of cogged wheels out of wood, powered by the running water of a stream – an early indicator of his propensity for Heraclitean logic, perhaps? In the late 1940s, looking to Marcel Duchamp's spinning works as a model, Tinguely devised a mechanism made from a high speed motor, an axle and a door mounted to the ceiling of his apartment in Basel. To this precarious device he would hang an array of objects – chairs, paintings, handbags, sculptures and so on. The machine would spin at high velocity until the objects attached would dematerialise, ultimately flung apart at great speed.

Considering his unorthodox domestic experiments, the incorporation of movement within Tinguely's work throughout the 1950s was relatively restrained, and did not fully appear until after his move to Paris in 1953. An early example, *Metamechanical Sculpture with Tripod,* 1954 (fig.2), consists of an iron tripod supporting a wire and cardboard construction. Seven wheels that function as cogs each

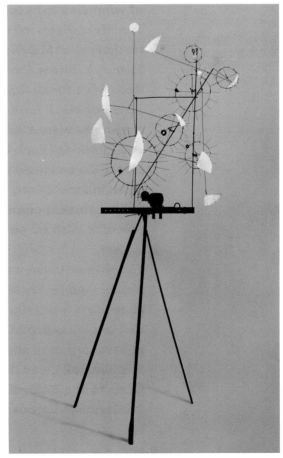

fig.2
Jean Tinguely
Metamechanical Sculpture with Tripod, 1954
236 x 81.5 x 91.5 cm

have further wire components to which eleven cardboard elements are attached at different spatial points, some mounted at right-angles. These planar devices, each cut from a circular shape, and painted white on one side and black on the other, provide spatial interruptions reminiscent of Calder and Malevich. Subsequent similar works are painted in bright primary colours, bearing an even closer resemblance to Calder's mobiles and to Malevich's Suprematist paintings. Some of the constructions are powered by hand-operated cranks, although Tinguely quickly progressed to the use of electric motors. *Metamechanical Sculpture with Tripod* has a motor mounted at the top of the tripod to power the structure, causing its wheels to rotate and move the system of interconnected parts. Such were Tinguely's flimsy constructive methods that some of the cogs regularly fail to turn or connect with adjacent parts, defining the entire structure, quite deliberately, as a system of unpredictability – the antithesis of the accepted logic of machines.

Tinguely's *Meta-Malevich* reliefs, made soon after, saw him embark upon a highly considered aesthetic sensibility and art-historical engagement that would be a defining characteristic of his work into the 1960s. More important, however, was a systematic progression of what was to become Tinguely's most significant 'material' – chance. The *Meta-Malevich* reliefs were, as their titles suggest, mechanised renderings of Malevich-esque paintings. They played upon the Russian's formulas, rather than specific works, alluding to his first pure abstractions – his *Black Square* set against a white background and the series of black monochromes, all first exhibited in 1915. Tinguely's responses were white, rectangular metal cut-outs set against black backgrounds. Each is individually mounted to a separate motor through a concealed connection at the rear of the black support; each turns independently and at its own speed. The result is a construction and motif that continually updates and modifies itself at random – a machine with no control as to its appearance at any given time.

The title of these works, prefaced by 'meta' is significant. The term was coined by Hultén following the rejection of the previously suggested 'mechanical sculptures', 'automata', or 'mobiles' which had proven unsatisfactory, particularly the last which was too close in association to the work of Calder. 'My suggestion was 'metamechanical, by analogy with 'metaphysical', and on one of my daily visits to the Bibliotèque Nationale I was able to check in the Grand Dictionnaire Larousse that 'meta' can be used to mean both 'with'

5
Ibid., p.16.

6
See Troels Andersen,
*The World as
Non-Objectivity:
Unpublished Writings
1922–25/K.S Malevich*,
translated by Xenia
Glowacki-Prus and
Edmund T. Little,
Copenhagen, Borgen,
1976.

and 'after' – which seemed just right. The association of ideas with words like 'metaphor' and 'metamorphosis' seemed to me to be very appropriate.'[5]

Ever changing, Tinguely's mechanical works occupy a state of paradox. On the one hand they exist according to their terms of reference, the strategies of modernism; on the other, they simultaneously undermine them. Malevich, for instance, considered the right-angles of his compositions to denote 'good' in the world, presenting his works as systems of spiritual and metaphysical explanation. Appropriating these angles, and Malevich's aesthetic, Tinguely added movement to the equation, thus inverting Malevich's (and modernism's) project, satirising it and transposing it to a new critical realm. Even the prefix 'meta' denies the original's potential to be a self-sufficient, self-referential object. It is revealing that both Malevich and Tinguely spoke of setting things 'free'. Malevich did so in terms of creating an art detached from the real world, the state and religion.[6] By contrast it was Tinguely's desire to unlatch art from the traditions of the modernist avant-garde, moving it closer to the real. His machines, and their chance-based unpredictability, mirrored the fluctuating rhythms of modern life and of technological advance.

The meta-mechanical works became increasingly elaborate. *Relief méta-mécanique sonore II*, 1955 (fig.3) was one of the first to incorporate sound as one element struck another (a 'ready-made' in the form of a bottle) and alluded, through its sequential movement, to some kind of specific functionality. Others further developed his earlier work in both extending and parodying the aesthetics of modernism such as *Wundermaschine, Méta-Kandinsky I*, 1956 (fig.11) and the supply elegant *Black and white relief méta-mécanique*, 1957 (fig.4).

fig.4
Jean Tinguely
Black and white relief
méta-mécanique, 1957
125 x 185.5 cm

All continued to embody chance as something experiential, a phenom-
enon to be witnessed live. Tinguely was of course not the first to
exploit chance in his work – Stéphane Mallarmé, Duchamp and John
Cage are clear examples – but the use he made of it is unique.

As would become increasingly apparent as the decade progressed,
particularly through his central role in the formation of the Nouveau
Réaliste group in Paris, Tinguely was turning ever more to the frenetic
energy and grittiness of contemporary urban life as an instigating
force – just as his neo-dada colleagues Robert Rauschenberg, Jasper
Johns and John Chamberlain were doing across the Atlantic. He
became ever engaged in the mechanised world and the relationship
between human and machine. Fascinated by new technologies, a
society of mass consumption and mass disposal, Tinguely and his
associates began to preserve and cerebrate it, addressing it on its
own terms – just as he had done with art history. By the close of the
decade there had, for some time, been an interplay in Tinguely's work
between the utilitarian and the functionless, and a tension between
the works as autonomous objects and their completion through

viewer interaction. Tinguely's concern for the implications of the machine upon society deepened with the start of a new and extensive series of works, the 'Meta-matic' drawing machines. These machines, the first of which was actually constructed in 1955, were numbered sequentially and first shown together at the Galerie Iris Clert, Paris in 1959 (fig.5). The last, *No.21*, was made in 1960.

Agents of mass production, the 'Meta-matics' varied significantly in scale and appearance – *No.14* and *No.15*, for example, were held and operated by hand, while *No.17* (fig.6), is over three metres high. But all had the same function: to make abstract drawings on paper. Human interaction, or rather collaboration, was once again a prerequisite. To make a drawing one first has to attach to a machine a blank sheet of white paper and then a biro or felt-tip pen, choosing its colour, before engaging its motor. The armature and clamp holding the pen then lurch into action, juddering over the page until the power is cut – either at the choice of the operator, or when the pre-set timer of the machine has been exhausted. The colour or type of drawing tool can be swapped midway through. The machines were a forceful critique of the dominant modes of artistic production at that time – *Tachisme* in Paris and Abstract Expressionism in the States. While such contemporaries laid claims to highly individual, emotive works that emerged spontaneously from the subconscious mind, Tinguely was offering machines that made perfectly acceptable abstract drawings on demand, time after time. Crucially, as the machines were subject

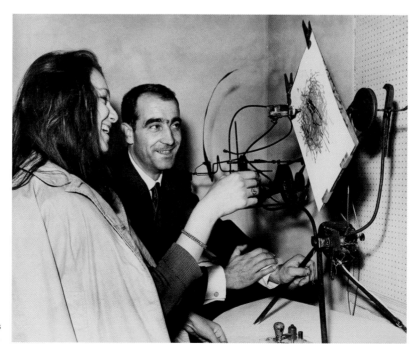

fig.5
Jean Tinguely with one of his
Meta-matic drawing machine

7
Richard Calvocoressi,
'Introduction', *Tinguely*,
The Tate Gallery, London,
1982, p.13.

8
Fredric Jameson,
*Postmodernism or, the
Cultural Logic of Late
Capitalism,* London and
New York, Verso, 1991,
p.73.

to a number of variables – type and positioning of paper and drawing tool, colour, pressure, time of operation and so on – no two drawings are ever the same. While on display at the first Paris Biennial in 1959, *Meta-matic No.17* reportedly made 40,000 unique drawings.[7]

But the critique went far beyond this. With his 'Meta-matics' Tinguely offered an alternative to humankind's power-struggle with the mechanised world. Machines are created to be superior to humans; to standardise production, to make or do things better, faster, cheaper, more frequently and with greater efficiency than ever possible by hand. We may be relied upon to invent, construct and even service machines, but essentially, once the 'on' switch is depressed, we are subservient. The disparity is enhanced when technology provides solutions to tasks or enables the creation of products simply unrealisable without them. Fredric Jameson provides a fitting analogy when discussing the daguerreotype process. Requiring the sitter, the person, to remain unnaturally still for the duration of the exposure, '[o]ne imagines the uncontrollable twitching of the facial muscles, for example, or the overwhelming urge to scratch or laugh.' An instant incompatibility between humankind and machine is thus revealed. To compensate, photographers 'devised something of the order of the electric chair, in which the heads of their portrait subjects, from the lowliest and most banal generals all the way to Lincoln himself, were clamped in place and immobilized from the back for the obligatory five or ten minutes of the exposure.'[8] Whether or not this is actually true – other accounts of the process suggest supports rather than immobilising 'clamps' – it reveals a need for a modification of behaviour when dealing with machines and technology. This potentially exaggerated description of an interaction between person and machine is also revealing in its conveyance of the myths and fears (strapped to an 'electric chair') that revolve around technology and are undoubtedly a feature of this time.

Tinguely's earlier machines obey only the laws of chance. By contrast his 'Meta-matic' machines follow rules created by their operator and, crucially, the operator can only act according to pre-determined limits of the machine. The play-off between the utilitarian and the functionless increased in scale and ambition in Tinguely's work as his career progressed. He presented an interaction between person and machine based upon mutual need, co-operation and 'respect': the chance for 'a game' that is potentially 'joyous' and 'free'. Subverting the entire logic of machines, and the fears often held over them, Tinguely

9
For thorough and highly informative descriptions of Tinguely's work post-1960 see Hultén, 1975 and Calvocoressi, pp.5–27 and the ensuing catalogue descriptions.

10
Michael Landy in 'A Conversation Between Michael Landy and James Lingwood', *Everything Must Go!*, London, Ridinghouse, 2008, p.103.

revealed an alternative way of managing one of the most fraught relationships that defined the mid-twentieth century.

Tinguely's machines became ever more theatrical and examples were produced that, among other things, smash full bottles of beer, throw balls, shake violently, destroy themselves, and explode into 'music' at the touch of a button.[9] When Michael Landy walked into that exhibition twenty-seven years ago, he was confronted by 'balls going into tunnels, po-going machines, abstract drawing making machines, machines that you could get on and ride.' His affinity with the artist at first came from his sense of humour – something Duchamp had also praised Tinguely for. Yet he was also struck by his use of materials. In contrast to his spacious studio today in which everything is confined to the surface of a lone trestle table, Landy at the time was an obsessive, yet un-rigorous, collector of junk: 'Smartie tops, old rusty bird cages, old billboard posters, chip forks, teddy bear eyes, hair combs, manhole covers, carpet underlay...my whole studio space was stuffed with junk. I wasn't a very discerning collector.' Landy saw Tinguely use these same societal discards, aestheticise them, and make them work as signifiers of wider social conditions and concerns. He was drawn to the ingenuity of his work, the inventive*ness* of his machines, particularly the 'Meta-matics' of the 1950s, and their potential for sociological critique.

In 1995, in the wake of Margaret Thatcher's leadership of the Conservative Government (1979–1990), Landy made *Scrapheap Services* (fig.7). Thatcher's labour market reforms – the acceleration of service industries and mine closures in particular – left vast swathes of society, especially men, out of work. Companies laid off significant numbers of staff, bowing to the growing pressure for ever-greater levels of efficiency and streamlined workforces as modes of production were increasingly mechanised and automated. During Thatcher's time in office unemployment rose to a level of more than one in ten. *Scrapheap Services* was offered as a waste-disposal solution; a system to remove the seemingly 'disposable' section of society who, without work, were state-dependent. The installation was conceived during a period of unemployment for Landy himself who, after signing-on and participating in a number of the Government's so-called 'back to work' schemes, decided to create employment for himself in the form of a 'cottage industry.'[10] The room-filling tableau consists of thousands of individual figures, a trained workforce with skills now obsolete, cut out by Landy from rubbish he collected over two

right:
fig.7
Michael Landy
Scrapheap Services, 1996

years – McDonald's burger cartons, Coke cans, cigarette packets and so on. Mannequins dressed in red 'Scrapheap Services' corporate uniforms, complete with logo, stand poised as they sweep up the figures, the dregs of society, collecting them into branded waste bins, rubbish carts and dustbin bags. A vast shredding machine, the 'Vulture', stands at the ready to dispose of them for good. The narration in the included promotional video declares:

Scrapheap Services consider it important that any people who are discarded are swiftly and efficiently cleared away, and this is part of our duty of care. Why put up with unsightly people who are such a burden on your resources when you can turn to the Scrapheap Services people-control range of products?

Scrapheap Services is one of the most scathing criticisms of Thatcher's time in office ever to have been made by an artist, yet with its clichés and parody manages to retain a humour worthy of Tinguely.

The work of Tinguely's that has had the greatest impact upon Landy is one that he could not have seen in the 1982 exhibition, for it no longer exists. While the 'Meta-matics' were machines of creation, Tinguely's concern for the processes, inventions and by-products of the age of consumerism led to a number of auto-destructive works – sculptures made with the specific purpose of destroying themselves. The most spectacular and influential of these was *Homage to New York,* a vast construction that came to life, and death, on the evening of March 17, 1960. *Homage,* one of the world's first ever 'happenings', was conceived as Tinguely travelled to New York onboard the Queen Elisabeth. He had complex ideas of the city, a place of which he had heard a great deal but had never visited. To him, it was where human-kind was closest to the machines it had created.[11] 'I saw in my mind's eye all those skyscrapers, those monster buildings, all that magnificent accumulation of human power and vitality, all that uneasiness, as though everyone were living on the edge of a precipice, and I thought how nice it would be to make a little machine there that would be conceived, like Chinese fireworks, in total anarchy and freedom.'[12]

The work was constructed with the help of Billy Klüver, an electrical engineer and founder of E.A.T.[13] After much persuasion, and with support from new-found friends in the city, Tinguely secured permission for the work to be realised in the sculpture garden of the Museum of Modern Art, a major coup considering how little known he was in

11
Calvin Tomkins, 'Jean Tinguely – Beyond the Machine', *The New Yorker*, February 10, 1962, reprinted in *Michael Landy H2NY*, Alexander and Bonin, New York and Thomas Dane Gallery, London, 2007, p.85.

12
Tinguely in Ibid., p.85.

13
E.A.T (Experiments in Art and Technology) was an influential organisation founded by Klüver and Fred Waldhauer, another engineer, along with Robert Rauschenberg and Robert Whitman in New York in 1967. Its purpose was to bring together artists and engineers to expand the role and possibilities of art in contemporary society. Following many of Tinguely's own concerns, it facilitated and promoted the integration of people with the technological age.

14
He had, at first, been declined permission after approaching Dorothy Miller, then a curator of MoMA's permanent collection. Miller informed Tinguely that it was the museum's role to 'preserve and conserve, and not to destroy art.' Tinguely then approached Peter Selz, who, being an exhibitions curator at the museum, understood and importance of temporary events. It was Selz who gained permission for the work to go ahead. Peter Selz interviewed by Michael Landy in Michael Landy, *H2NY* (documentary film), Britdoc, London, 2009.

15
Billy Klüver, 'The Garden Party', reprinted in Hultén, 1975, p.130.

America at the time.[14] MoMA offered him a Buckminster Fuller dome, left from a previous exhibition, to use as his studio. This technological promise of a utopian existence was a fitting context given Fuller's and Tinguely's shared concern for the welfare of society. In stark contrast to the slick, futuristic aesthetic of the dome, however, Tinguely turned to his usual materials and spent many days plundering the junk yards and scrap merchants of the city. Klüver was also sent off on regular missions to obtain specific parts or asked to invent new things to be added. Constructed in several sections, *Homage* was to perform and unravel sequentially as a play, a piece of music or a narrative, as it slowly obliterated itself in front of a live audience.

Over the next three weeks an extraordinary array of junk was accumulated and brought to the dome for assembly under Tinguely's instruction – sixty or more bicycle and baby-carriage wheels, a meteorological balloon, a piano, a bassinet, tin cans, a cable drum, sheet metal, a washing machine drum, pulleys, an addressograph machine and various motors along with chemical smoke and smells provided by Klüver. The first section to be completed included a large vertical 'Meta-matic', the bassinet and a pot and drum which were to provide percussion – the pot was struck by a nut and the drum 'attacked' by the motor from a fan.[15] A second was completed around the piano, to which ten armatures, all assembled from various bicycle parts, were attached and rigged to periodically strike its keys. Another 'Meta-matic' was also added, along with a radio which had been sawn in half, and dozens of the wheels. Two scrolling text machines, one vertical and one horizontal, were entrusted to Herbert Migdoll, an intern at the museum. Tinguely told him that he could write whatever he wanted on the paper that would come out of them. Anticipating his moment of fame, Migdoll spelt out his name repeatedly on one and concluded his contribution with the word 'PENIS'.

The meteorological balloon was inflated and positioned atop a pole that towered over the structure, making it now over eight metres high (Tinguely anticipated it bursting toward the end of the performance and drooping forlornly over the rest of the structure). Two further elements were added in the final stages that would detach themselves from the main structure and take on, as Tinguely's machines so often did, a life of their own. One, equipped with a powerful motor, was fitted with a klaxon and set on wheels. At a specific point the device was to jettison itself from the 'mother-ship' and hurtle into the crowd, dragging several other objects with it. Another less obstreperous

16
Ibid., p.136.

17
Ibid.

18
Calvin Tomkins quoting
Sylvester in *H2NY*
documentary.

19
Klüver in Hultén, 1975,
p.136.

22

device made from an oil can and cable drum, completed with the American flag, was to 'move laboriously' in a different direction.[16] When the time came it was to toss itself into the pond and commit suicide, drowning beneath the fittingly mournful gaze of Aristide Maillol's *The River* (completed 1943). The entire machine was to follow suit. The steel tubing that was largely supporting the structure was engineered by Klüver to steadily collapse – although there was no time, and perhaps no inclination on Tinguely's part, for testing. The joints were designed to melt from the heat of overpowered resistors once electrical power was connected. As Klüver wrote:

> *As the first 'Meta-matic' collapsed, it would fall backward. The piano, placed on a frame two feet above ground, would itself fall backward into the fallen meta-matic. The second 'Meta-matic' and the support for the balloon would be dragged along by the fall of the piano. Behind the piano, Jean mounted a carbon-dioxide fire extinguisher, concealed by wooden boards. As a lever was pulled the extinguisher would empty itself with a big swoosh. At the same time, the bell on the Addressograph would begin to ring.'* [17]

The evening of the performance came with fanfare. MoMA sent invitations to the press and to the city's great and good. Mark Rothko, Philip Guston, John Cage, Robert Rauschenberg (who had contributed a money-throwing device to be included in the structure) and Governor and Mrs Rockefeller were all in attendance, as was David Sylvester, who left early muttering something like 'I don't like tuxedo Dada' when the machine failed to start on time.[19] Ever conscious of his audience and for the aesthetics of his work, on the night before the destruction took place Tinguely made the decision to paint the entire construction in white to give an aesthetic unity – a serene order that contrasted with the disorder of its demise. Such visual unification turned the whole thing into a relief, a move that linked the structure to many of his previous works. Looking, in part, like an enormous meta-Malevich and including 'Meta-matics', sound, movement and a fusion of the creative and the destructive, *Homage* was something of a mid-career retrospective for the artist, bringing together his endeavours to date.

An hour after planned, Tinguely made his final adjustments and signalled for the power to be connected – 'the construction and the beginning of the destruction were indistinguishable' Klüver said.[19] The machine juddered to life, although of course all did not go according to plan and almost straight away a fuse blew. Klüver got it working again and the event commenced. Although the audience knew something of the deleterious nature of the event, they were also expecting the machine to do something functional. In some ways it did, sporadically, but in characteristic fashion the action occurred according to the terms of the machine and not of those who had created it. The many wheels began to turn and the large 'Meta-matic' started up, but Tinguely had accidently reversed the flow of its paper – it moved up instead of down – and he had even forgotten to connect the motor to power the drawing arm. He laughed. A bucket of petrol that had been installed turned over at the right moment, emptying itself onto a flame on the piano which started to burn. Klüver's smoke began to billow out of the machine and was blown into the crowd by an electric fan, but his chemical stinks failed to release. The percussive elements also worked, as did the radio, but only three eery notes from the piano could be heard, repeating themselves over and over. The klaxon device, which had also caught fire, shot out at great speed aiming itself at a photographer standing on a ladder. Obligingly, he dismounted, caught the machine and sent it on its way, straight towards the sound equipment of NBC who had come to record the event. The 'suicide carriage' was less successful and faded long before it ever reached the pond.

After twenty minutes or so the structure had began to sag heavily, but was clearly never going to fully collapse. By this point the fire in the piano was burning fiercely and spreading. Tinguely became concerned that the fire extinguisher concealed within it would explode from the heat and began to talk to the awaiting fire department. After some debate, and reluctance on their part because of all the electrical components, they took the decision for the flames, and for the *Homage to New York*, to be extinguished. The crowd booed, blaming the fireman, and after only 27 minutes the event was over. *Homage* had 'failed to fail', Calvin Tomkins was to say later, and had to be brought back under control by human hand.

Dore Ashton, art historian and then a critic for *The New York Times*, witnessed the entire performance, writing an invaluable blow-by-blow account that is reprinted in this volume. *Homage to New York* now lives on only in such reports, in photographs and in two exceptional films – one by the artist Robert Breer and a documentary by D. A. Pennebaker. Perhaps against the original spirit of the occasion, a number of 'relics' of the machine still exist, now scattered around the

20
At the time of construc-
tion Tinguely wanted all
parts of the machine to
be destroyed, and the
remains discarded in the
same way that they were
found. Nevertheless he
took great delight in the
audience's stampede to
collect souvenirs at the
end of the performance
and ended up signing
some of the 'relics'
several years later.

21
Vance Packard,
The Waste Makers,
Harmondsworth and
Ringwood, Penguin,
1960.

fig.8
Artforum magazine
advertisement, 2007

world.[20] Tinguely's was the ultimate comment on American society and consumerism, working both with and against its metropolis backdrop. It was a celebration of modern life; of the machine, of technology, of commerce and of production. Mimicking the pace and fluctuations of contemporary urban living, its ingenuity, parody and susceptibility to chance and failure were devices used once again by Tinguely to address fears about a new age at the start of a new decade. That same year, Vance Packard published 'The Waste Makers', his damning attack on American consumer culture.[21] The titles of its chapters say it all: 'The Nagging Prospects of Saturation', 'Progress through the Throw-Away Spirit, 'Progress through Planned Obsolescence', 'How to Outmode a $4,000 Vehicle in Two Years', 'The Changing American Character' and so on. Tinguely took great delight in the various failures of the machine, and contrary to much writing on the work, it is unlikely that he was saddened by the mode of the machine's ultimate demise. As ever, chance, fate, change and unpredictability took over – the only constants in life.

Landy has a long-standing desire to recreate *Homage* and present it to new audiences fifty years later, a posthumous continuation of Tinguely's collaborative spirit across time and space. He has spent considerable time researching the work in MoMA's archives and those of the Museum Jean Tinguely, Basel, studying films, photographs and promotional materials. He even initiated a search for its 'relics' through an advertisement in *Artforum* magazine (fig.8). Yet any such re-enactment can only be inaccurate. Elements of the structure, its operations and multiple 'failures', remain as unknowable today as they were even to Tinguely at the time. Such slippage would, however, perversely ensure a truthfulness to its original, being as susceptible to the peculiarities of fact and history as its model was to happenstance. That said, the realisation of *H2NY*, as Landy calls it, would see him make the ultimate homage to Tinguely, ensuring the machine is destroyed, for good, under its own terms rather than by human intervention. That's the plan, anyway – but we know what happens to those.

As part of his investigations Landy has made 160 or more drawings and a documentary film in response to *Homage*. Working from photographs taken during the performance, the drawings are completed either in white on black, directly after Tinguely's painted structure, or as a negative in black on white. Methodically executed with his customary dexterity, the meticulous detail of the drawings has allowed

Landy almost to step into the shoes of his hero, transporting him to the moment of the machine's creation and operation. Until the moment arrives when all the relevant permissions may be obtained for him to begin, these drawings – part celebration, part research – are as close as he can get to the real thing. As things currently stand, however, it is with another work, perhaps the most extraordinary of Landy's career to date, that Tinguely's influence can be most clearly felt.

If *Homage* was defining of its times in 1960, Landy's *Break Down* (figs.9 and 10) was to be the same in 2001. The previous year he began to catalogue everything he owned, from his passport and birth certificate to the masses of stuff accumulated over the years of his existence. His toaster, kettle, furniture, clothes, car, video player, books, childhood belongings, cutlery, records – all 7,227 of his worldly goods – were itemised and sorted into categories. After the success of *Scrapheap Services,* which technically resulted in Landy's gainful employment as an artist and gave him a new-found disposable income, he wondered how he could 'mess everything up.'[22] His conclusion was to destroy everything on this list.

For *Break Down,* Landy took over the vacated C&A department store in the commercial zenith that is London's Oxford Street for two weeks.

22
Michael Landy in
*The Man Who
Destroyed Everything,*
BBC Television, 2004.

fig.9
Michael Landy
Break Down, 2001

fig.10
Michael Landy
Break Down, 2001

23
Michael Landy in 'A
Production Line of
Destruction: Parts of
a Discussion between
Michael Landy and
Julian Stallabrass',
*Michael Landy/Break
Down*, Gerrie van Noord
(ed), Artangel, London,
2001, p.109.

Working with a team of 'operatives' he created his own machine, a
part conveyer-belt, part assembly line, that paraded his belongings
to a passing, and often unwitting, audience – the store was open and
accessible to all, just as any other on the street. Each object was
ultimately to be fed into an industrial shredder, a kind of grown-up
version of that which had appeared in *Scrapheap Services*. What
was so significant about the process, however, was that rather than
simply launch his belongings onto this path of destruction, Landy
worked first with his team to systematically disassemble every object:
the forces and processes of destruction were thus employed to reveal
those of creation. His car, a Saab 900, was taken apart piece by piece
by a mechanic. Electrical items were unscrewed and reduced to their
component parts and clothes were un-stitched and separated. These
'products' were taken back to the start of their life, reduced as
near possible to raw materials. Landy created a 'production line of
destruction', making what he called 'the ultimate consumer choice'.[23]
He regained power from manufacturers that so often create objects
with a built-in obsolescence. But Landy is himself also a manufac-
turer, and all his previous artwork, the markers of professional life,
were also destroyed (he even included a drawing he had made on
one of Tinguely's 'Meta-matic' machines in the Tate exhibition).
Everything that travelled on the conveyer-belt was ultimately treated

and classified as a consumer object as Landy literally pulled apart the mechanisms of consumerism, and indeed those of the art market.

Visitor reaction was important to *Break Down,* as it was for *Homage.* Tinguely spoke of wanting the audience to fall in love with his machine so they felt an empathy once they began to witness its demise. He spoke of it almost as a person, somewhat romantically proclaiming the machine to be 'a marvellous thing. It's a sculpture, it's a picture maker...it's a componist [composer], it's a poet.'[24] As Landy's belongings passed in front of his audience he was conscious of their desire to take something for themselves, or that they would recognise 'something they've just bought, that they have in their carrier bags.'[25] Yet he was determined that everything, once obliterated in the shredder, would be taken to a landfill (or 'Landy-fill' as he later called it). No trace of his prior existence would be retained.[26] Similarly, Tinguely and Klüver agreed that *Homage* 'should be one continuous process – out of the chaos of the dump and back again.'[27]

With *Homage to New York* and *Break Down,* Tinguely and Landy respectively made two of the most forceful examinations of consumerism, waste, destruction and creativity in pre- and post-industrial society. Both works, living on only in memory, documentation, rumour and myth, became the ultimate in dematerialised sculptures of their age. Using the waste of their times they revealed that the pleasure of consumption, it seems, can also lie in its destruction.

24
Tinguely interviewed in D.A. Pennebaker's documentary film *Breaking It Up at the Museum,* 1960.

25
Landy in van Noord, p.108. Landy also liked the idea that when people came in from Oxford Street, one of Europe's biggest shopping streets, that they would continue acting like shoppers, browsing the objects.

26
Landy in *The Man Who Destroyed Everything,* op. cit.

27
Klüver in Tomkins, 2007, p.88.

fig.11
Jean Tinguely
Wundermaschine,
Méta-Kandinsky I, 1956
39.8 x 103.2 x 33 cm

THE MUSEUM OF MODERN ART, NEW YORK

The Department of Painting and Sculpture Exhibitions

invites you to witness

HOMAGE TO NEW YORK

A self destroying work of art conceived and built

for this occasion

by Jean Tinguely

Thursday, March 17 at 6:30 p.m.

R.S.V.P. Circle 5-8900 - Ext 247

This invitation will admit two

Mr. Tinguely's construction will be on view from
5 p.m. The spectacle will begin at 6:30 and will
take approximately 30 minutes.

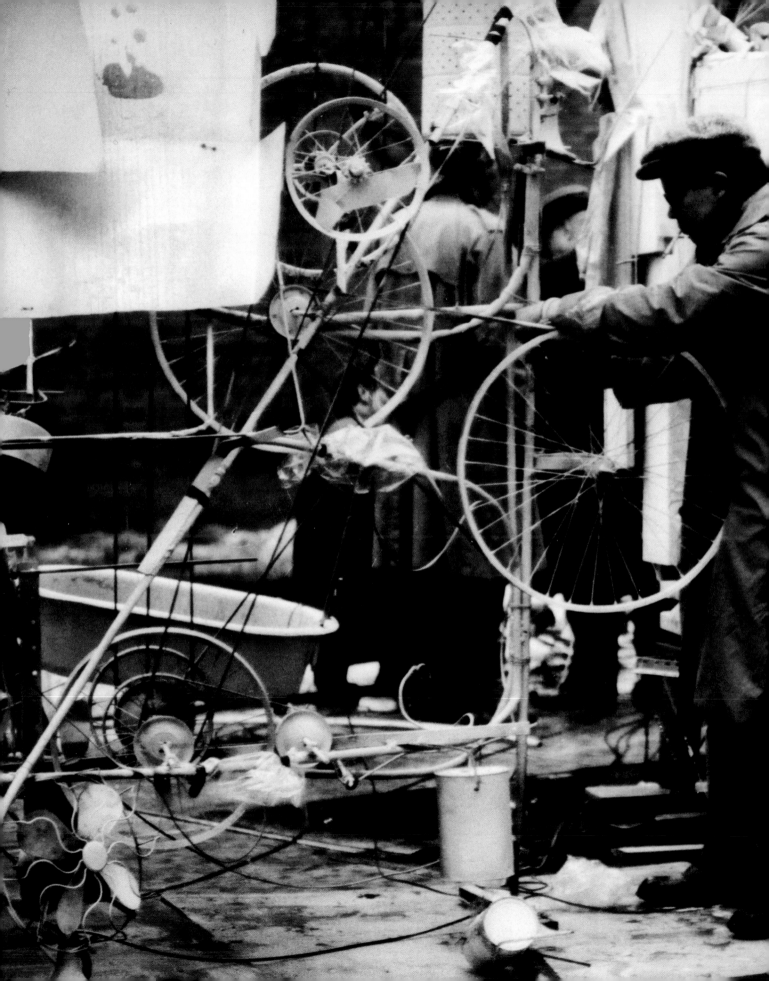

Log, March 17, 1960

Dore Ashton

10:00 am
A bitter rain, but event scheduled anyway.

3:00 pm
I call S. He says they are having a hell of a time. The men assisting T.
to install the machine – there are about five separate units, with fifteen
motors and a control box and scientific assistants standing by – think
it is junk and treat it accordingly.

4:15
Still cold, raining. The garden is gray and slushy. Two museum
fonctionnaires stand under umbrellas forlornly watching a frantic
sawing. At the last minute, the museum worried about its marble
flag-stones. Blocks of wood must be placed under the machines.
The Emperor not in sight yet.

Balzac rain-slicked and lowering.

4:30
Rain stops. Camera men aimless. They look like they are covering the
war in Korea. Begins to look like movie set. Gaping faces in cafeteria.
T. tinkering with the worried expression of an airplane mechanic
making the last check-up on the Emperor's plane that is taking the
Emperor behind the iron curtain where if everything doesn't go right,
what a responsibility.

4:40
Rain again. They mount the weather balloon sagging like a mariner's
flag in the doldrums. In the glass hall in front of the cafeteria three
black-cloaked gentlemen look gravely into the garden. They are
disapproving artists.

5:00
S. tells me Mathias Goeritz is distributing leaflets against the demon-
stration. He is talking about God and morality. They say he is serious.

5:30

Photographers on roof; on first, on second, on third floors; and in the Whitney. Shouting up and shouting down. David Sylvester, British art critic, very soberly appears to leave: 'Don't like tuxedo dada.'

6:00

The fourth machine installed and T. goes up ladder to put a huge roll of paper on the large drawing machine. An actress next to me says T. is cute. Remarks 'This thing is certainly hung up with the press.' Yells. Cameramen, Huelsenbeck stands in a puddle. Finally gets a discarded piece of lumber to put under his feet. Someone near T. is reading instructions and examining the control board. T. mounts ladder and oils or inks the sponge that will draw.

6:20

Nothing happens, nothing at all.

6:30

Actress chats with Kenneth Tynan. 'I've seen plays like this, self-destroying' says he. Someone puts a canvas bag with airline's insignia on Maillol's lady. St. John has a klieg-light at his feet.

6.45

T. puts some plastic tape near the paper roll. Without plastic tape what could be done in this world? Who's paying for this says an irate voice to my left.

6.48

Test piano briefly. Rustle in crowd. Suspense, suspense, suspense.

6:50

Raining again. T. comes from dome with baby machine cradled in his arms. It has wheels and a long klaxon.

6:51

Sawing. T. puts large bottles in the gutter running above the largest machine. They are supposed to roll down and break, Rauschenberg with a Florida tan hands T. more junk.

6:56

Yellow smoke! T. runs back. From the wings the leading actor appears: a blue-capped, blue-garbed, blue-eyes Fireman. The Fireman is

suffering. A look of consternation never leaves his face. Like the Fireman in the *Bald Soprano*, he doesn't know why he is there.

7:10
The flaccid balloon writhes, struggling to catch its breath. A camera-man perched on a ladder looks trepidantly at bottles poised to explode. Suspense.

Supposing T. really *is* an anarchist and plans to blow us all up. He is an anarchist. It says so in the broadsheet. Voice: "I'll tell my wife I missed the commuter's train because I watched a machine destroy itself. She's never heard *that* one before."

7:12 Voice:
"Pity General De Gaulle isn't here."

7:13
The roustabouts take away excess lumber. A kewpie-doll child appears silhouetted in a high window opposite.

7:15
Inquiring reporter with his own little machine with its own plastic tape helps the super-machine. Mr. Tynan, he asks, what is your impression. Er. Well. I'd say it was the end of civilization as we know it. Perhaps the entire thing is a hoax. Across the street there may be eighteen machine guns waiting.

7:18
"You been to one of these things before?"
"I've seen the coronation in London."

7:20
The balloon lumbers bumpily on, the machines are in situ, jet plane overhead, everyone cold and damp, a bottle of cognac lasts only five minutes.

7:30
Like all drama critics, Tynan leaves before the third act.

7:32
Piano plunks. A small flame appears. The Fireman waits. The fan starts whirring, the paper, ... the paper rolls itself up the wrong way.

Crowd laughs then groans. They still think the machines are intended to function. Smoke billows, we can see nothing for three minutes, But the piano clunks out its three notes. A string breaks, a wheel falls off. The crowd is disturbed. T. goes to the controls and consults with worried collaborator. The museum *fonctionnaires* move in. Something is wrong.

7:37

I can't read the text. All I see is the word 'hope'. They say it ended with the word penis. It then wound itself back up. The toy wagon attached to a wheel bobs up and down like an oil drill.

7:38

I catch 4 words of text: Now is the foe. Fire eats with relish. More flames. The drumming machines doesn't seem to work. The flapping paper flirts with the flames reaching avidly for it. Next machine. Orange smoke, wheels turning, a bell, ding. Two more cans fall.

7:50

Piano really burning now. Two boys with fire extinguishers appear. T. seen arguing with Fireman. Crowd thinks *fonctionnaires* interferes. They loath his silver buttons. No, no, no, they call, booing the Fireman. Ding. T.'s assistant goes over to machine, leaps back, electric-shocked.

7:55

Drawing machines making Chinese mountains. The hoses turned on full blast. Flags wave madly. A baby machines in flames skitters towards the audience. Screams. Someone grabs its torso and sends it flaming back toward T. Ding. Ding.

8:00

Fireman disputes. Runs into the museum. Returns trundling a giant fire extinguisher. A look of iron determination on his face. Boos. Meanwhile, the second-largest machine with the piano is overturned and lies smoldering. The crowd still feels betrayed. Something is wrong. Voice: 'This is like an unfinished nightmare.'

8:05

T. assists one of the smaller machines to limp off-stage. Smokes belches intermittently. Cameras, cameras, and suddenly in the confusion, the thing seems to be at an end. Milling. Finally T., smiling, faces cameras. Cheers, bravos. What has happened or not happed no one can be sure. T. says he instructed them to put out one part of the fire. The Museum says it never knew there would be a fire. The *fonctionnaire*, whines: 'I dunno if I done the right thing.'

Extract taken from 'Prologue and Log',
first published in *Arts & Architecture*, May, 1960

44

Michael Landy
H2NY Homage to
New York, 2007
153 x 244 cm

Michael Landy
H2NY Tinguely Tinkers, 2006
21 x 29.8 cm

Michael Landy
H2NY Theatre of Junk, 2007
59.3 x 83.9 cm

Jean Tinguely
Fragment from *Homage to New York* (text machine), 1960

Michael Landy
H2NY An Unbeautiful Joke with No Punch Line, 2007
83.9 x 59.3 cm

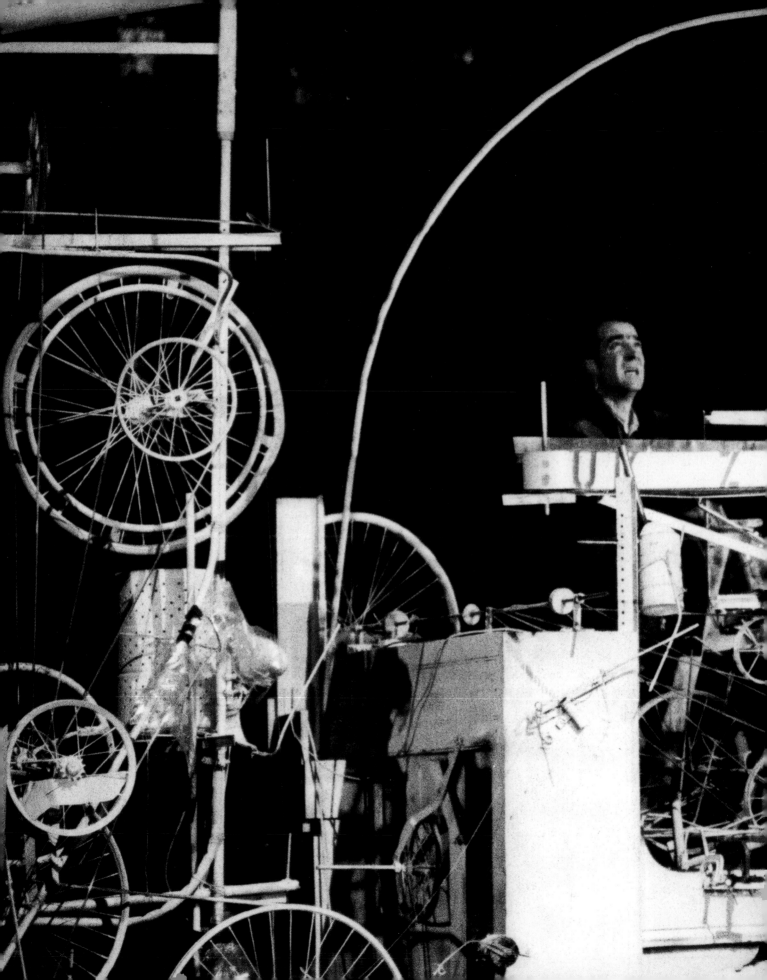

Homage to New York

We know that emotion cannot be petrified, that love
cannot be bound, that life cannot be conserved and
time cannot be held. Jean Tinguely's experiments are
works of art in which time, movement and gesture are
demonstrated—not merely evoked. Tinguely accepts
the Heraclitan change inherent in life. His is a world
in flux and constant self-transformation.
Being very much part of his time, Tinguely uses machines
to show movement, but he is fully aware that machines
are no more permanent than life itself. Their time runs
out, they destroy themselves. This he demonstrates
dramatically in *Homage to New York*. Here he brings
the motor into an ironic situation which controverts its
function. Rendered helpless, it no longer operates in
its normal way. It destroys itself more quickly because
it performs more intensely.
In New York Tinguely finds a maximum concentration of
human life and energy, a virility which accelerates its
own dissolution. He believes that the idea of a self-
constructing and self-destroying mechanized sculpture
would never have occurred to him in the ancient
ambiance of the Mediterranean coast. Its dynamic
energy as well as its final self-destruction—are they
not artistic equivalents for our own culture?
He has conceived and built this sculpture and is
eager to witness its loss so that we may witness
its choreography.

PETER SELZ
(taken from announcement to *Homage to New York*, 1960)

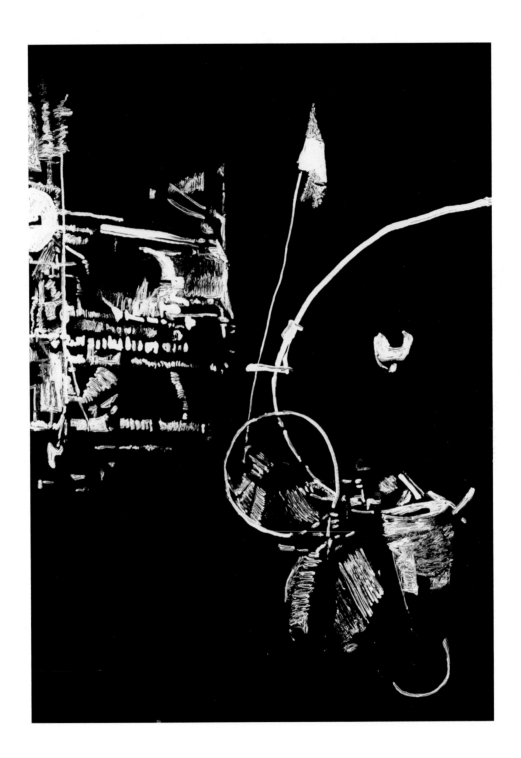

Michael Landy
H2NY Sorcerer's Apprentice, 2006
29.8 x 21 cm

Michael Landy
H2NY Mr Tinguely Makes Fools of Machines, 2006
101.6 x 66.7 cm

Tinguely ex machina

Forty years ago Tinguely's grandadas thumbed their noses at Mona Lisa and Cézanne. Recently Tinguely himself has devised machines which shatter the placid shells of Arp's immaculate eggs, machines which at the drop of a coin scribble a moustache on the automatistic Muse of abstract expressionism, and (wipe that smile off your face) an apocalyptic far-out breakthrough which, it is said, clinks and clanks, tingles and tangles, whirrs and buzzes, grinds and creaks, whistles and pops itself into a katabolic Götterdämmerung of junk and scrap. Oh great brotherhood of Jules Verne, Paul Klee, Sandy Calder, Leonardo da Vinci, Rube Goldberg, Marcel Duchamp, Piranesi, Man Ray, Picabia, Filippo Morghen, are you with it?

TINGVELY EX MACHINA
MORITVRI TE SALVTAMVS

ALFRED H. BARR, JR.
(taken from announcement to *Homage to New York*, 1960)

Robert Rauschenberg
Fragment from *Homage to New York* (money thrower), 1960

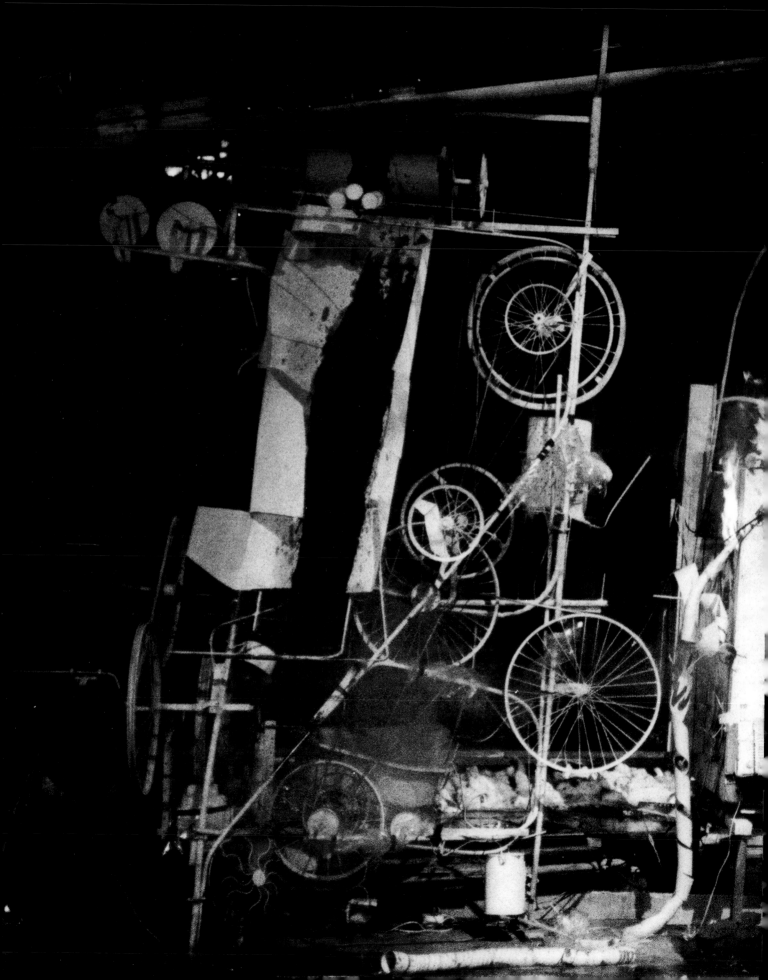

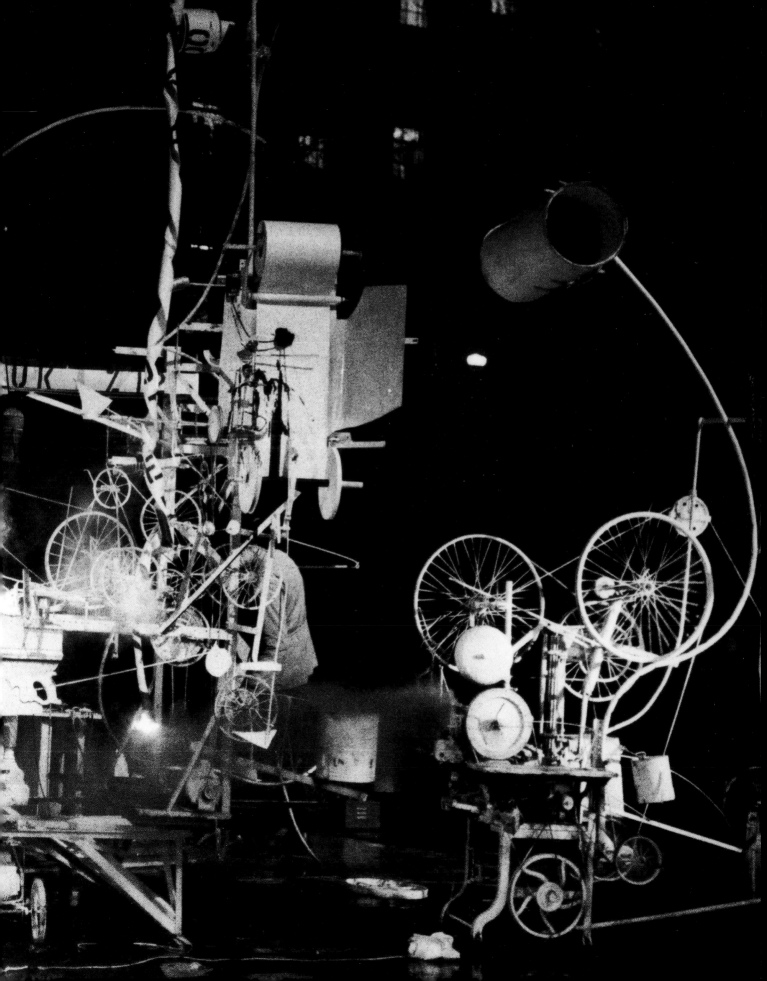

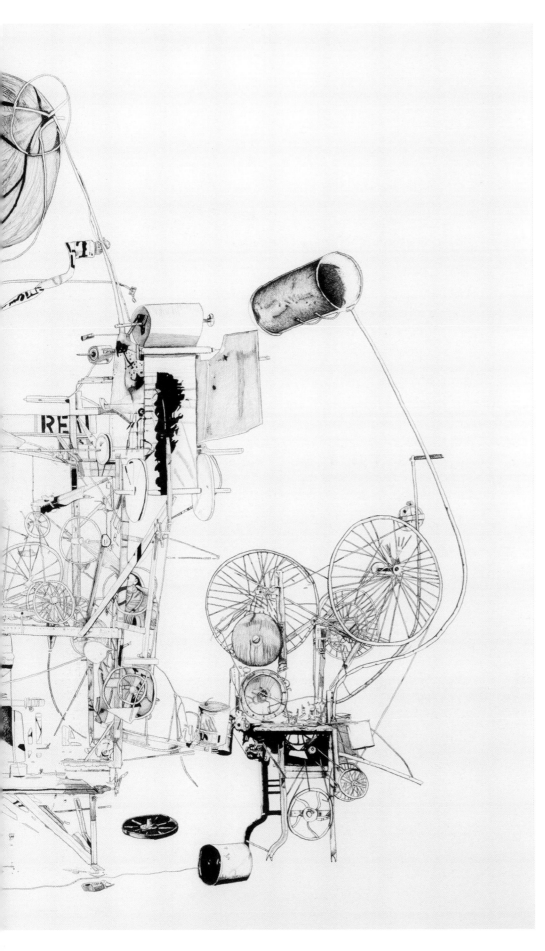

Michael Landy
H2NY Self-constructing,
Self-destroying Tinguely
Machine, Museum of Modern
Art, 17th March 1960, 2006
150 x 227 cm

Tinguely's things are so good that maybe they are not modern art any more. In place of regularity he puts irregularity. His machines are not machines, they are anti-machines. They are mechanic and meta-mechanic. They make anarchy. These things are more free than a human being can ever hope to be. They represent a freedom that whithout them would not exist. They are pieces of life that have jumped out of the systems: out of good and bad, beauty and ugliness, right and wrong. To try to conserve the situation that exists will make a man unhappy, because it is hopeless. This kind of art accepts changes, destruction, construction and chance, that rules anyway. These machines are pure rhythm, jazz-machines. But look out, because it is not an innocent game.

K.G. Hulten
(taken from announcement to *Homage to New York*, 1960)

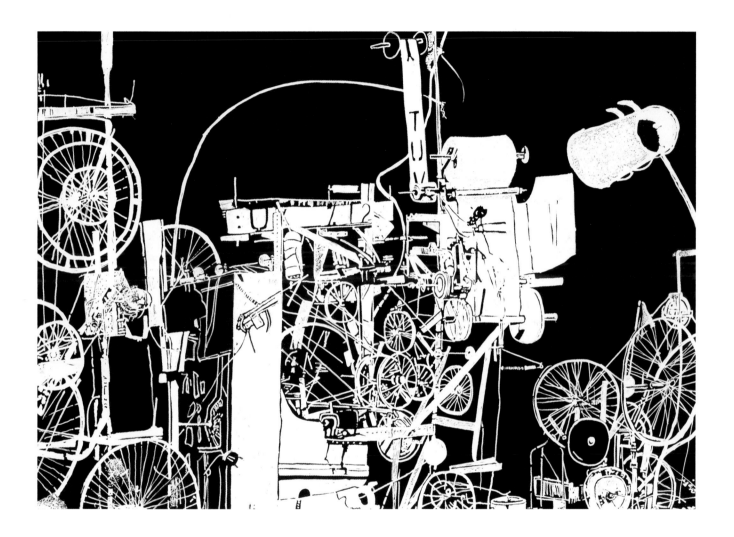

Michael Landy
H2NY Three Piano Notes, 2006
59 x 84 cm

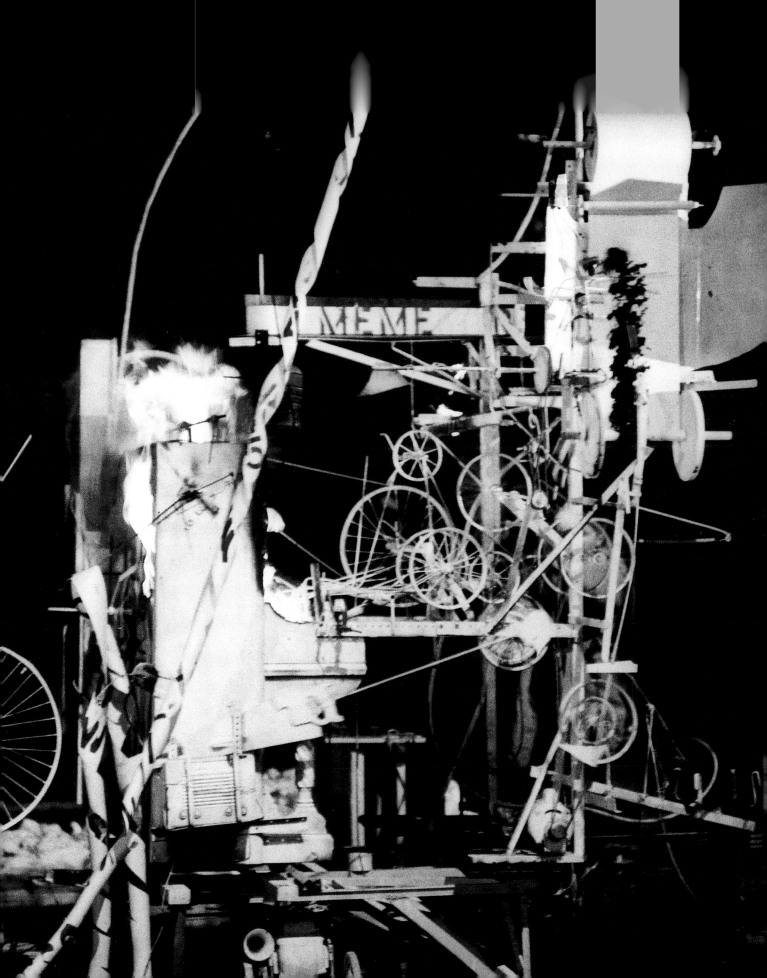

Michael Landy
H2NY Tinguely Machine Beats Itself into Fiery Frenzy, 2006
30 x 42 cm

Michael Landy
H2NY Large Meta-matic, 2006
42 x 30 cm

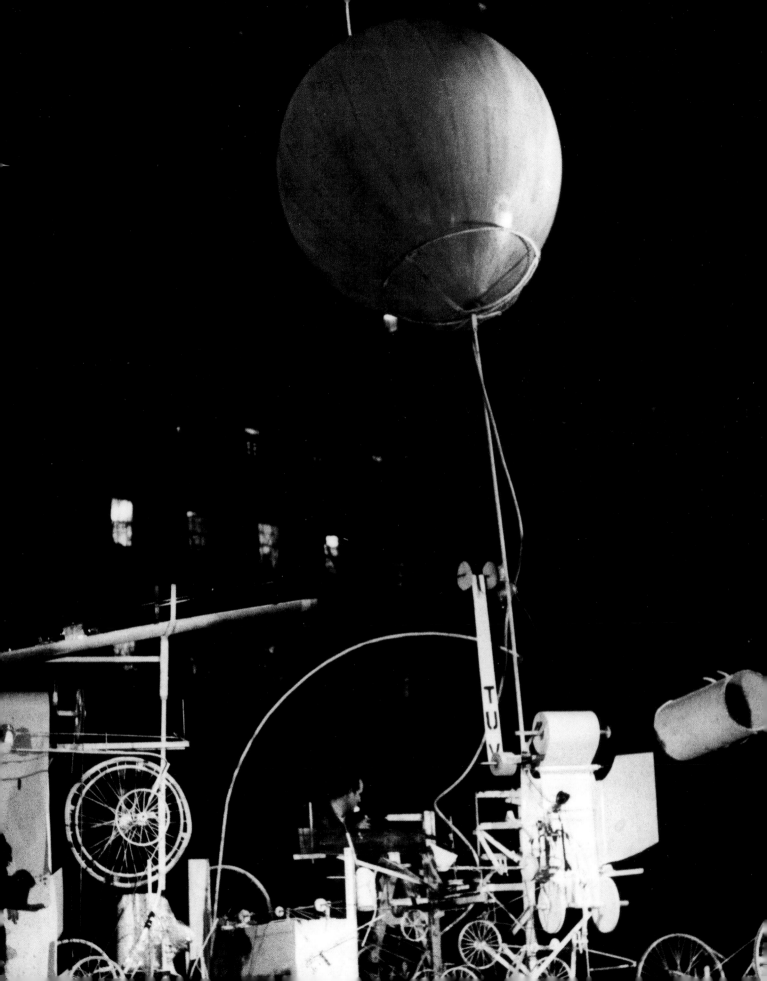

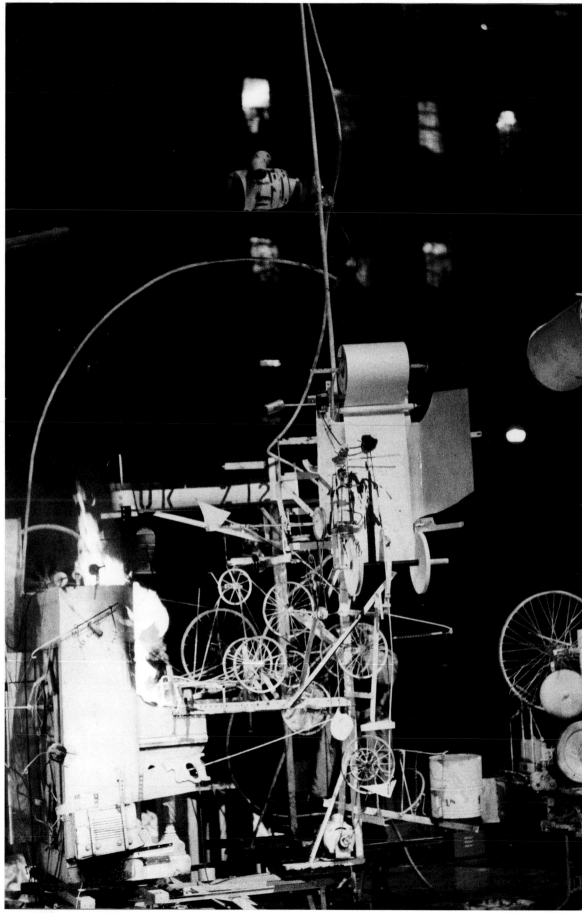

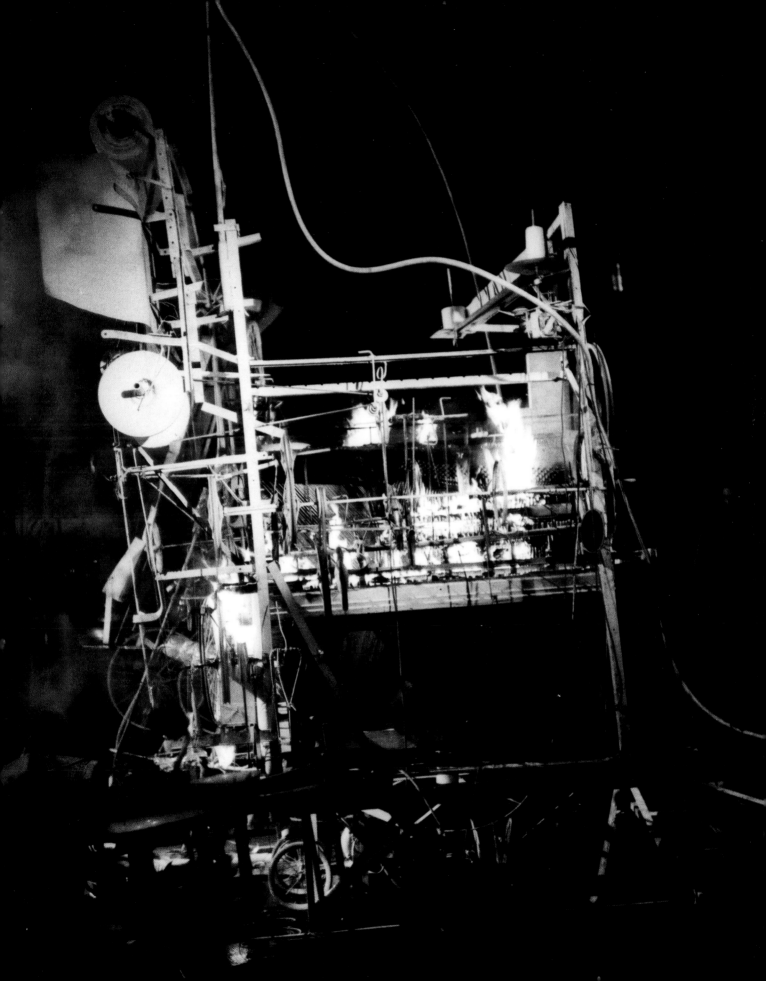

Michael Landy
H2NY Self-constructing, Self-destroying, 2006
152.5 x 122 cm

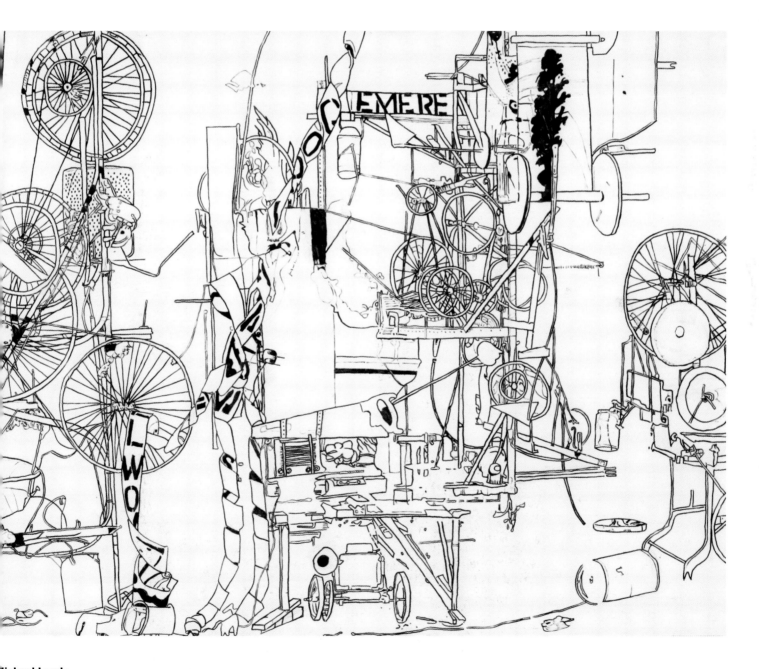

Michael Landy
2NY Blazing Sculpture 'Watered Down', The Stars and Stripes, 2006
22 x 153 cm

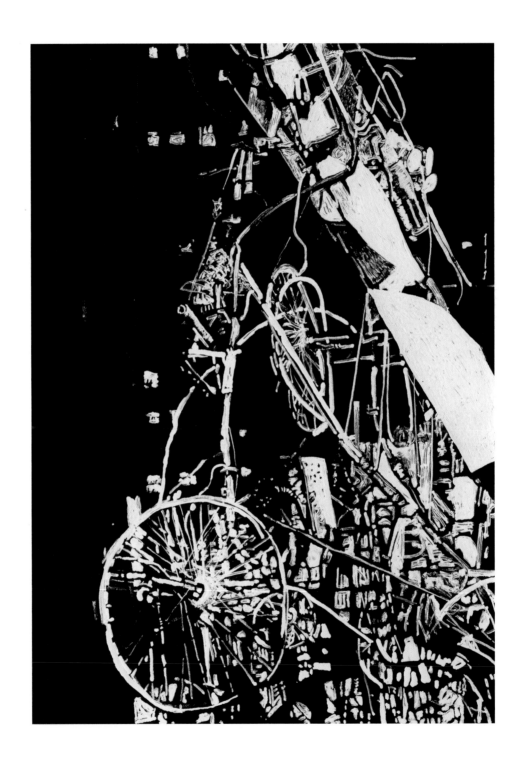

Michael Landy
H2NY Fantasy Machine, 2006
29.8 x 21 cm

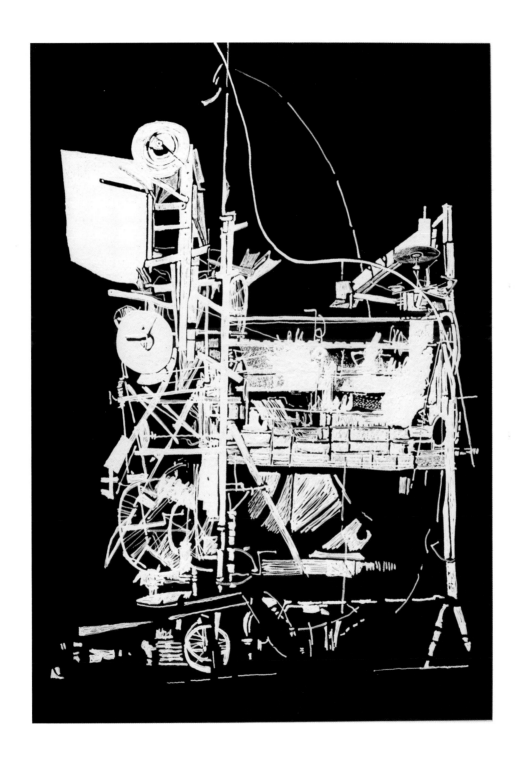

Michael Landy
H2NY Their Time Rubs Out, They Destroy Themselves, 2007
83.9 x 59.3 cm

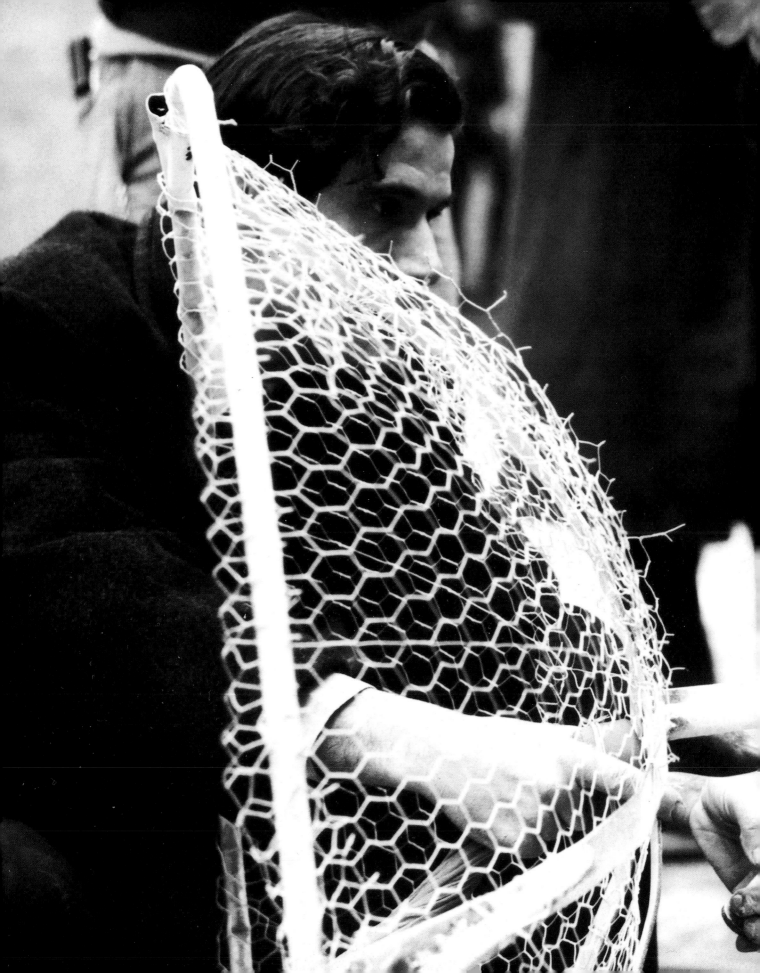

There are times in human history when the things men have been accustomed to doing and have long accepted as a part of the established order erupt in their faces. This is the situation right now——the universal crisis is forcing us to redefine our cultural values. We are like the man who is astonished to discover that the suit he has on does not fit him any longer. Religion, ethics, and art have all transcended themselves, especially art, which, instead of being art as we know it, has come to demonstrate man's attitude toward his basic problems. So it is senseless to ask whether or not Tinguely's machines are art. What they show in a very significant way is man's struggle for survival in a scientific world. There are two kinds of art, if we may still use the word "classicistic" art that relies on tradition and Dada art that relies on shock for its effects. I would call Tinguely a Meta–Dadaist because his machines not only turn traditional concepts upside down but also realize the old Dada love of movement. Tinguely is the inventor of the perpetuum mobile. I think his work is one of the great breakthroughs in modern art. It is a giant step toward *la realité nouvelle.*

RICHARD HUELSENBECK
(taken from announcement to *Homage to New York,* 1960)

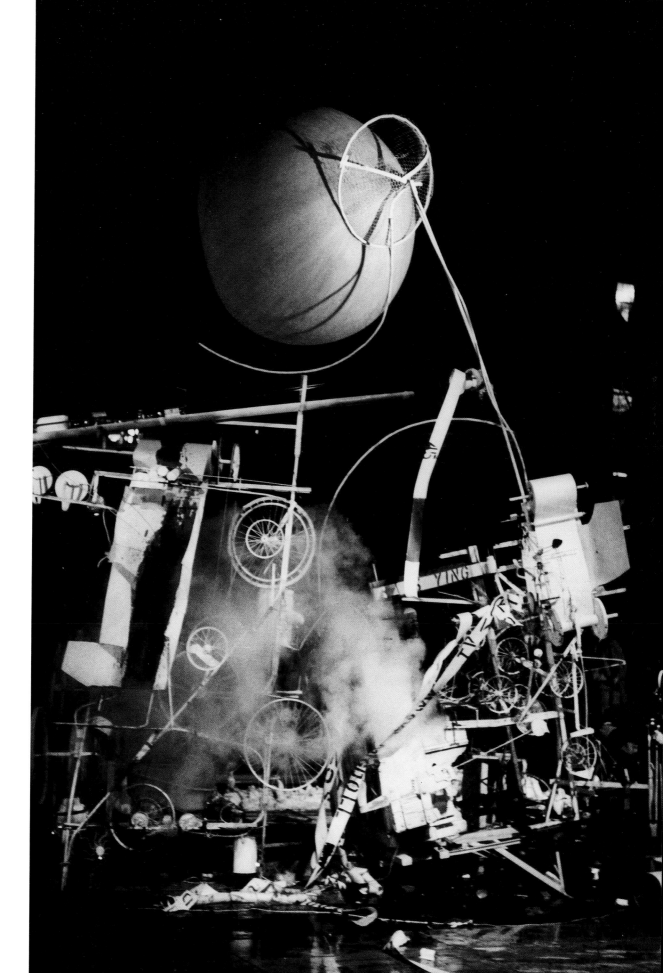

Jean Tinguely
Drawing for *Homage to New York*, 1960

Michael Landy
H2NY Futile Ends, 2007
83.9 x 59.3 cm

Michael Landy
H2NY Kinetic Apparition, 2006
122 x 152.5 cm

PLEASE STOP!

STOP the aesthetic, so-called "profound" jokes! STOP boring us with another sample of ego-centric folk art! All this is becoming pure vanity!

Today it is Jean Tinguely who wants to make us believe that his HOMAGE TO NEW YORK is leading us to a "wonderful and absolute reality". But we discover that nothing has happened since the decisive moments of Dada. It is still the same miserable, neurotic reality which fortunately never became absolute. It is not true that what we need is to "accept instability". That is again the easy way. We need STATIC VALUES!

Of course it is difficult to believe, since GOD was declared dead. It became easier to live without GOD, without cathedrals, without love. Nonconformism is easier to face than the Bible; functional vulgarity easier than cathedrals; sex easier than love. And — as the easy way became fashionable — our whole modern art is in a sad situation.

It is a fact that man is not made only to rationalize. Man is also made to believe. When man believes, he becomes able to do more important work.

We need faith! We need love! We need GOD! GOD means life! We need the very definite laws and commandments of GOD! We need cathedrals and pyramids! We need a greater, a meaningful art! We do not need another easy self-destruction.

Be consequent! Honor the tradition of Hugo Ball! Go forward and make the decisive, the most difficult step of Huelsenbeck's NEW MAN: From Dada — to faith!

Responsible for the text: Mathias Goeritz

Mathias Goeritz
'Please Stop' announcement in protest against *Homage to New York,* **1960**

Michael Landy
H2NY Picture Making Machine II, **2006**
152 x 122 cm

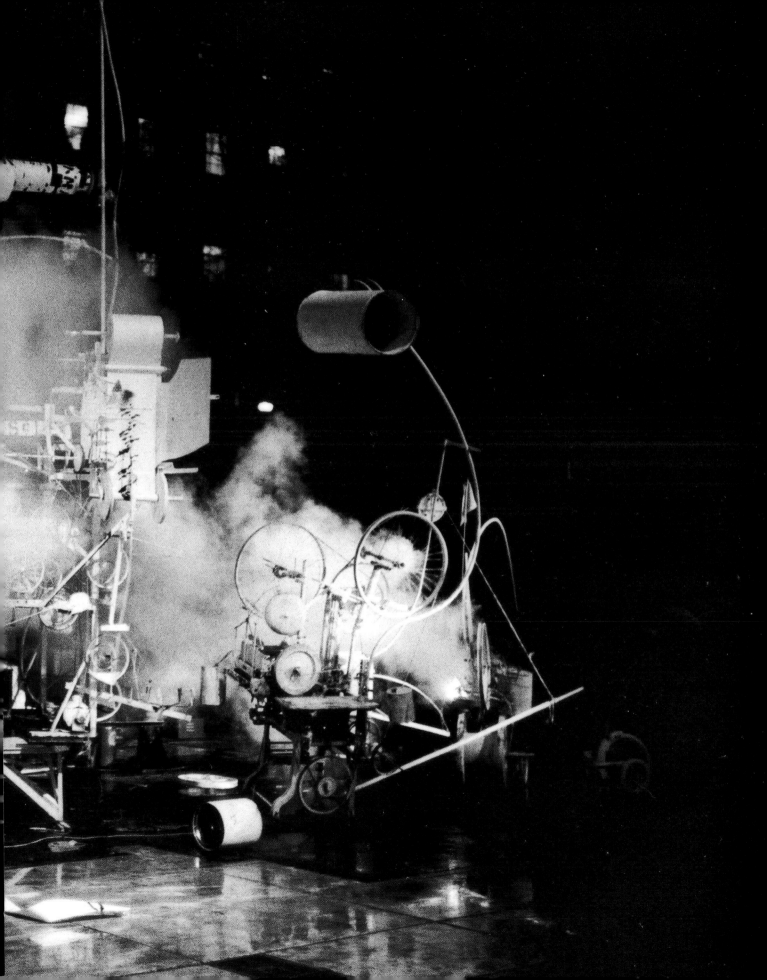

Michael Landy
H2NY Self-destroying Sculpture Garden, 2006
70 x 81 cm

H₂N.Y. Self-destroying Sculpture Garden
Michael Landy 2006

Michael Landy
H2NY The Audience Gave a Rousing Cheer for the Dying Monster, 2006
30 x 42 cm

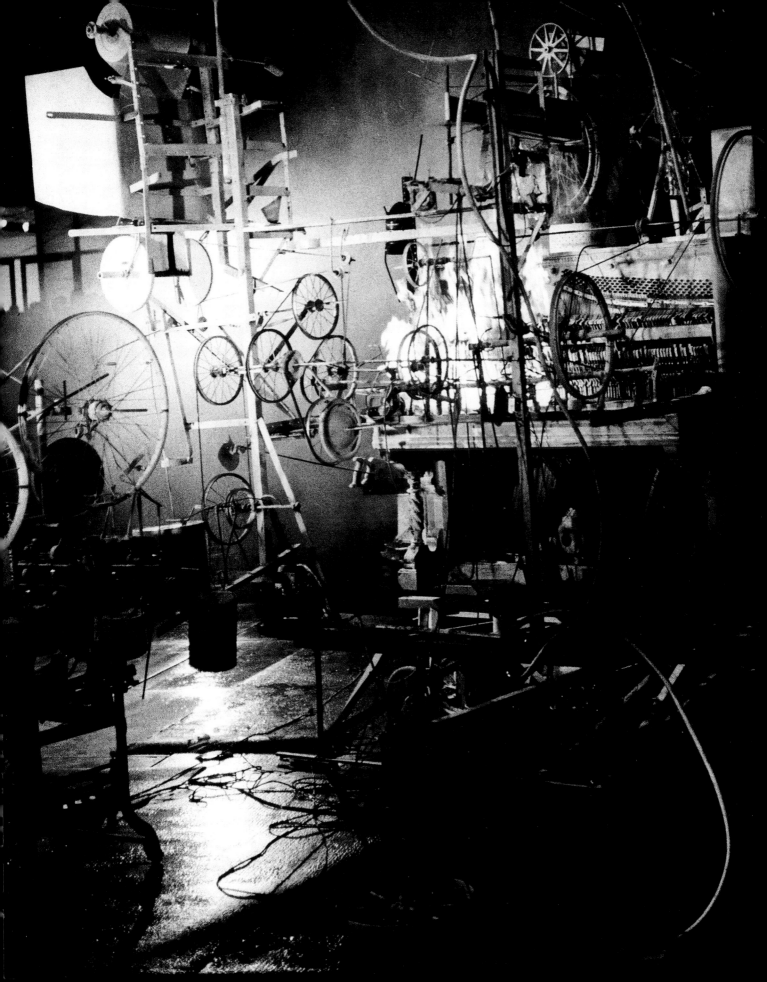

Michael Landy
H2NY Metallic Suicide, 2006
152 x 122 cm

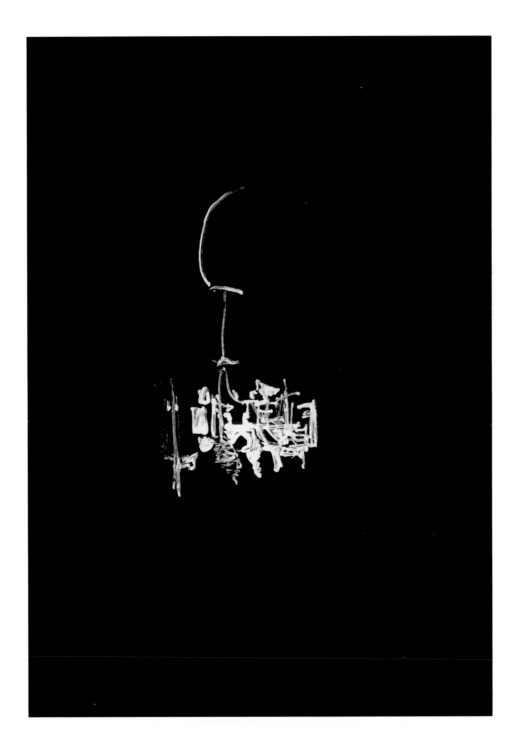

Michael Landy
H2NY Inorganic Ending, 2006
30 x 21 cm

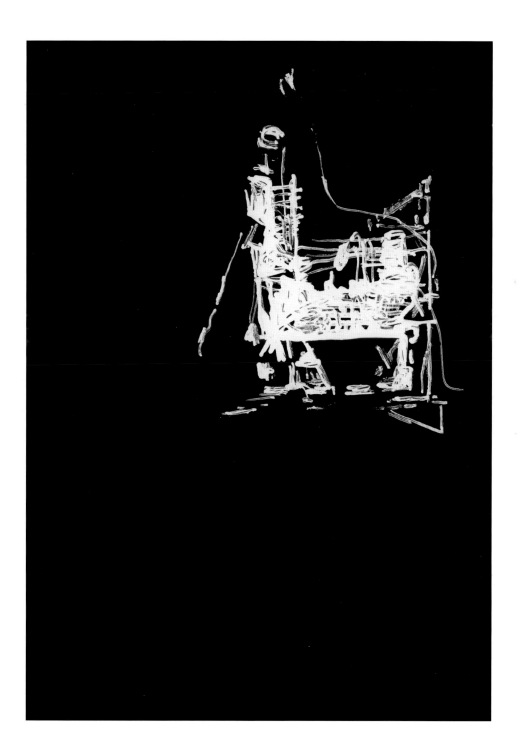

Michael Landy
H2NY The Notes Played Wistfully Out of Tune, 2006
59.3 x 83.9 cm

Tinguely's art is:

—An art of spectacle—without the boggling crowd
these machines would no more exist than Hegel's
orchid in the jungle.

—An art of artlessness and imperfections—more
human than machine.

—An art of destruction enacted—not concealed and
held captive as they are in "ordinary" painting.

—An art of movement that at its very limits touches
fixity—*les extrêmes se touchent.*

DORE ASHTON
(taken from announcement to *Homage to New York*, 1960)

110

Michael Landy
H2NY Apocalyptic Far Out Breakthrough, 2007
122 x 153 cm

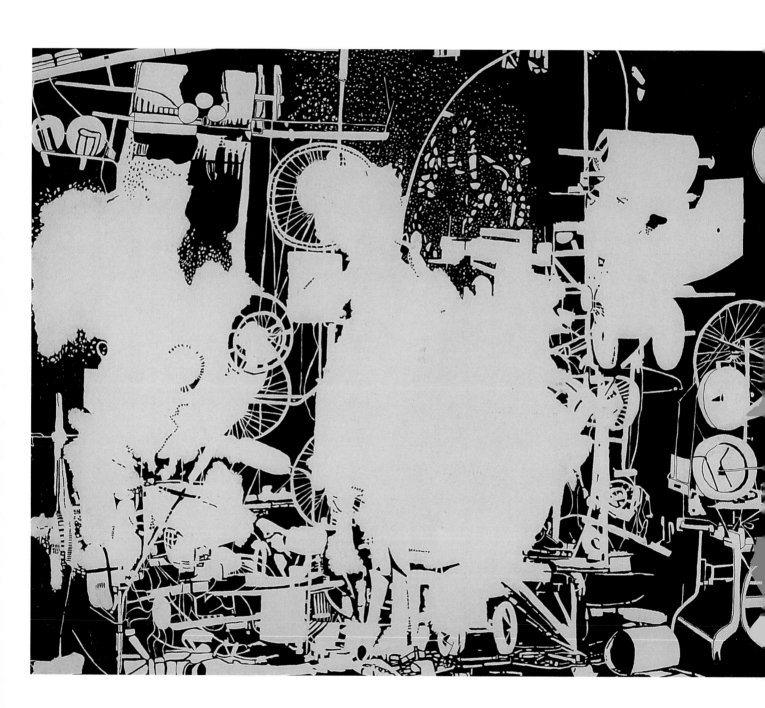

Michael Landy
H2NY Tinguely's Self-destroying Sculpture Drowns Itself in Maillol's 'The River' 2007
122 x 304 cm

The Fire

The fire was damped and Bob Breer
courageously knocked the supporting
pieces of wood from under the piano
— Tompkins — Tinguely suddenly began
to worry fore fear the fire extinguis
-her in the piano would explode
from the heat, and he wanted firemen
to put out the blaze. Kluver found
a fireman in attendance, who seemed
to be enjoying the show. He listened
to Kluver pleading and then with
apparent reluctance, signalled to two
museum guards, who ran out with
small extinguishers and applied them
to the piano fire. — A Times photogra
-pher who went inside the museum
a few minutes later overheard the
firemen talking to headquarters on
the telephone. "There are these machines,
see," he was saying, "and one of
them is on fire, but they tell me it's
a work of art, see, and then this
guy tells me himself to put it out,
see, and the crowd yells "No! No!"

Michael Landy
H2NY The Fire, 2006
30 x 42 cm

Michael Landy
H2NY Machine Comedy with Ironic Ending, 2006
29.8 x 42 cm

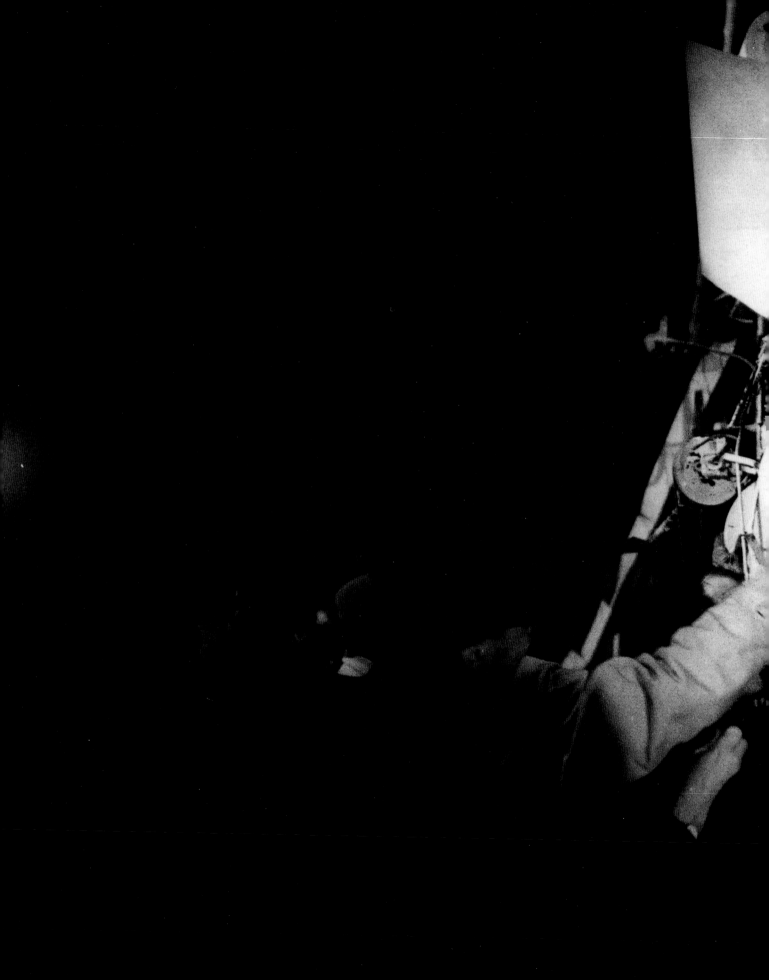

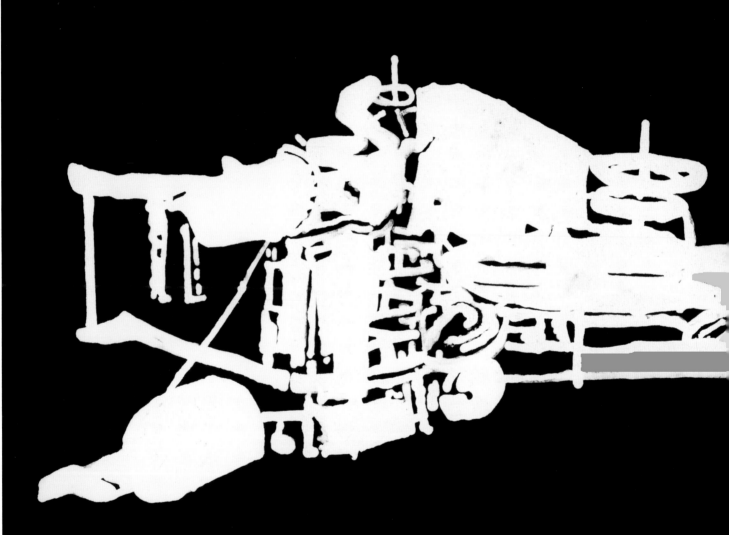

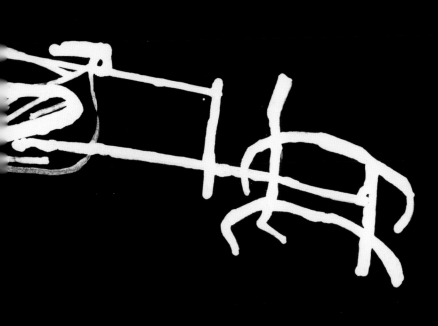

Michael Landy
H2NY Addressograph Machine Lays Dying, 2006
30 x 42 cm

si la scie scie la scie
et si la scie qui scie la scie
est la scie que scie la scie
il y a Suissscide métallique.

Marcel Duchamp
1960

1960

Marcel Duchamp
'Swiss Suicide', on announcement to *Homage to New York*, 1960

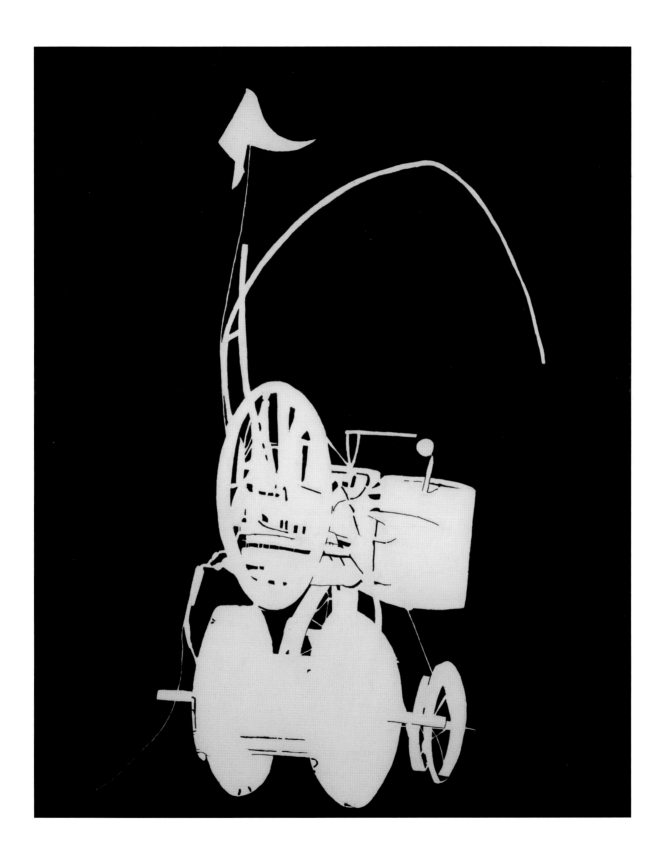

Michael Landy
H2NY Suicide Carriage Breaks Down, 2007
152 x 122 cm

Jean Tinguely
Fragment from *Homage to New York* (suicide carriage), 1960
203.7 x 75.1 x 223.2 cm

Heavy Meta: Landy and Tinguely in the Dump

Michael Landy

*'Once in my life I would like to own something outright before it's broken!
I'm always in a race with the junkyard! I just finish paying for the car
and it's on its last legs. The refrigerator consumes belts like a goddam
maniac. They times those things. They time them so when you've finally
paid for the them, they're used up'*
Willy Loman in Arthur Miller's *'Death of a Salesman'*

Michael
So why are we standing on this huge rubbish dump in New Jersey?

Jean
We have been transported back in time to help me collect junk for
Homage to New York which will commence at 6.30 pm on 17 March
1960 in the Sculpture Garden of the Museum of Modern Art, New York.

Pass those bicycle wheels, child's go-cart and bottles of chemical
stinks. The stinks will come in handy they will fall down from the
trough near the end of the performance, and hopefully stink out the
garden for days afterwards.

Michael
Tell me more about *Homage to New York*?

Jean
It is my spontaneous response to New York City, which I am visiting
for the first time, the skyscrapers, those monsters buildings all that
magnificent accumulation of human power. I want to escape the
material limits of sculpture by building something akin to Chinese
fireworks, which will exist only for a short period of time in total
anarchy and freedom. When I first arrived from Paris on the Queen

*Landy and Tinguely
Collecting Junk on
the Dump, 2009*

Elisabeth, I said that the whole machine must end up in the garbage cans of the museum.

Michael
That's funny because your work normally comes from the dump and mine ends up there.

Jean
Some bits of *Homage to New York* did escape the dump, parts were broken off by souvenir hunters at the end of the performance and they asked me to autograph them. The largest piece that survived the carnage was my Suicide Carriage, an odd looking contraption which travelled a few yards before breaking down during the event. It was supposed to drown itself by Aristide Maillol's *The River*, unfortunately it didn't because I attached a second-hand motor to the machine. It is now in the collection of the Museum of Modern Art, even though I don't recognise it as an artwork.

Michael
Look I found a bucket of gasoline, broken radio and an old addressograph machine.
Talking about junk, John Scanlan's book *On Garbage* states, 'The thing is that matter goes on, it never really disappears, but instead takes on different forms. What looks like a glistening object at one time eventually ends up in a pile of crap. This is the fate of all things.'

Jean
Yes, that is their fate, until you're armed with an acetylene torch.

Michael
I wonder what you would have created with your magical torch if you had discovered all my 5.75 tonnes of shredded possessions on this dump after *Break Down*, especially interesting is what you would have made of the Holy Water from our Lady's shrine in Knock.

Jean
I would have sprinkled Holy Water onto your deceased belongings to bring them back to life.

Michael
That's a strange coincidence since that's what I want to do. I like the idea of reconstructing *Homage to New York*, which only lasted for

27 minutes some 50 years ago. Its sole purpose of existence was to destroy itself, which it ultimately failed to do. So it was left up to the New York Fire Brigade to put it out of its misery.
Did you ever pay the fine that the fire chief issued you with at the end of the performance?

Jean
Yes, I used Robert Rauschenberg's silver dollar coins from his Money Thrower.

Michael
I visited your retrospective exhibition at the Tate Gallery in 1982 and came away with my own do-it-yourself Meta-Matic drawing, which subsequently I destroyed during *Break Down*. You have previously talked about *Homage to New York* avoiding being museumised, so I just wondered how you felt then about the existence of Museum Jean Tinguely in Basel which seems to be at odds with the ethos of your work?

Jean
And this is the main reason why I summoned you to the dump. I want you to break into the museum and construct a machine out of the parts of my sculptures, dating up until 1960. The machine will be created to destroy the Jean Tinguely Museum and the rubble from the ruin should be used for gravestones for auto-destructive artists.

Michael
Look you're standing on a meteorological balloon.

Jean
That's good, the balloon can burst and hang disgustingly over the machine at the end of the performance.

Michael
Let's talk more about *Homage*. It took you three weeks to construct in the Buckminster Fuller Dome with the help of a Swedish engineer called Billy Klüver.
Why did you decide at the last moment to paint the self-mutilating machine white, which by this time measured 23 x 27 feet high?

Jean
I wanted to make it beautiful, so when it destroyed itself there would

be a real sense of tragedy. Members of the audience cried, they wanted the machine to be preserved somehow. The day of the event it snowed and I became concerned the snow would detract from my machine, so I asked the workmen to paint the snow black, which they refused to do (laughs).

Why don't you go out and build your own self-destroying machine?

Michael
But what is the point of building something from zero when I already have a perfectly good model to work from. I also like the idea that *Homage to New York* returns as a kinetic apparition once a year on St Patrick's Day and performs for the permanent bronze sculptures in the museum's garden.

Jean
Just found an old upright piano, jar of titanium tetrachloride and washing machine drum.

I feel we both share a common interest in creation and destruction of value.

Michael
That's good. And what's the meta for?

We also share an interest in 'the machine' – but tackle it in polar opposites. My efficient machines, which appear in *Scrapheap Services* and *Break Down*, and your contraptions, which are more human in their behaviour.

I read somewhere that you said 'those whose jobs it is to destroy are often happier than those who have to build.'

Jean
Well in *Homage to New York* I managed to combine the two, I wonder if some of the junk we are collecting will move from no value to something of worth.

Michael
I hardly think this bedraggled American flag or baby's bassinet classifies as an antique. But then again, if the baby's bassinet escapes this junkyard, plays a part in *Homage to New York,* and is taken away as a memento, it could reappear years later as valuable remnant in a New York auction house.

List of Works

Height precedes width
precedes depth

138

Jean Tinguely

Composition 1947
Komposition
Oil on canvas
41 x 56 cm
Museum Tinguely, Basel

Composition 1949
Komposition
Oil on canvas
38 x 54.5 cm
Museum Tinguely, Basel

Detached Element I 1954
Relief Méta-mécanique
Tubular steel frame, steel wire,
cardboard, electric motor
81 x 131 x 35.5 cm
Museum Tinguely, Basel

Méta-Malevich 1954
Relief Méta-mécanique
Wood, metal, rubber belt,
electric motor
61.5 x 49 x 10 cm
Galerie Ziegler SA, Zurich

Méta-Malevich 1954
Relief Méta-mécanique
Wood, metal, rubber belt,
electric motor
40 x 40 x 8 cm
Musée d'Art Moderne de la
Ville de Paris

Méta-Malevich 1954
Relief Méta-mécanique
Wood, metal, rubber belt,
electric motor
61 x 50 x 20 cm
Museum Tinguely, Basel

Méta-Malevich '6 Barres Décallées'
1954–56
*Relief Méta-mécanique 'A Daniel
Spoerri-Feinstein'*
Wood, metal, rubber belt,
electric motor
59 x 49 x 20 cm
Weserburg | Museum für moderne
Kunst, Bremen, Sammlung Karl
Gerstner

*Metamechanical Sculpture with
Tripod* 1954
Méta-mécanique à trépied
Board and metal
236 x 81.5 x 91.5 cm
Tate. Purchased 1984

Prayer IV 1954
Moulin à Prière IV
Metal wire and rods, electric motor,
black wooden base
71 x 50 x 30 cm
Private Collection. Courtesy Galerie
Reckermann, Cologne

*Sketch for Méta-Malevich –
Méta-mechanical Sculpture* 1954
Black ink and pencil on paper
21 x 27 cm
Museum Tinguely, Basel

*Sketch for Méta-Malevich –
Méta-mechanical Sculpture* 1954
Black ink and pencil on paper
21 x 27 cm
Museum Tinguely, Basel

*Sketch of Méta-Malevich Function
and Movement* c.1954
Black ink on paper
13.6 x 21 cm
Museum Tinguely, Basel

*Sketch of Méta-Malevich Function
and Movement* c.1954
Black ink on paper
13.5 x 21 cm
Museum Tinguely, Basel

*Sketch of a Sculpture on Wheels,
Showing Features and Movements*
c.1954
Black ink on paper
27 x 21 cm
Museum Tinguely, Basel

*Sketch showing Function and
Movement with Plexiglass Wall
Construction* c.1954
Black ink on paper
21 x 27 cm
Museum Tinguely, Basel

Barometer / Transmission 1955
Méta-Malevich / Radskizzen
Pencil on paper
27 x 21 cm
Museum Tinguely, Basel

Blanc – blanc + ombre 1955
Relief Méta-mécanique
Wood, painted metal, rubber belt,
electric motor
60.5 x 48.5 x 17 cm
Galerie Ziegler SA, Zurich

Blanc sur Blanc 1955
Relief Méta-mécanique
Wood, painted metal, rubber belt,
electric motor
74.5 x 57 x 19 cm
Museum of Fine Arts Berne,
Anne-Marie and Victor Loeb
Foundation, Berne

Design for Méta-mechanical Relief
c.1955/58
Black ink on paper
13 x 9 cm
Museum Tinguely, Basel

Design for Méta-mechanical Relief
c.1955/58
Black ink on paper
13.8 x 27 cm
Museum Tinguely, Basel

Drawing Machine No.3 1955
Machine à dessiner No.3
Black painted panel, metal disc,
wire; rear, wooden wheels, rubber
belts, electric motor
54.5 x 106 x 33 cm
Museum Tinguely, Basel

Drawing made by Méta-matic No.1
1955
Black, orange and red felt-tip pen
on paper
Diameter 64.5 cm
Museum Tinguely, Basel

Méta-matic No.1 1955
Metal, paper, felt-tip pen,
electric motor
96 x 85 x 44 cm
Centre Georges Pompidou, Paris;
Purchased 1976

Méta-mécanique 1955
Méta-mechanische skulpturen
Painted metal, wire, electric motor
89 x 82 x 65 cm
Museum Tinguely, Basel

Page from sketchbook with drawing
for Méta-méchanical sculpture
c.1955
Black ink on paper
13.5 x 9.2 cm
Museum Tinguely, Basel

Relief Méta-mécanique
(blue, noir, blanc) 1955
Pencil and gouache on paper
7 x 21 cm
Museum Tinguely, Basel/Donation
Niki de Saint Phalle

Relief Méta-mécanique Sonore II
1955
Relief Méta-mécanique
Black painted panel with white
painted cardboard elements, metal
and wire, bottles, funnel, saw and
electric motors
73 x 360 x 48 cm
Museum Tinguely, Basel

Salut Pontus – Billet – Gabo – Man
Ray – Munari 1955
Black ink with envelope and
excerpts from a tool catalogue
13.5 x 21 cm
Museum Tinguely, Basel

Sketch for Meta-mechanical Sculpture
and Relief c.1955
Blue ink on paper
28 x 22 cm
Museum Tinguely, Basel

Sketch of Méta-mechanical Sculpture
Function and Movement c.1955
Black ink on paper
13.6 x 21 cm
Museum Tinguely, Basel

Sketch Showing Functions and
Movements for 'Living Painting'
c.1955
Black ink on paper
13.6 x 21 cm
Museum Tinguely, Basel

Untitled c.1955
Oil, acrylic paint and oil pastel
on paper mounted on cardboard
21.1 x 27 cm
Centre Georges Pompidou, Paris;
Purchased 1988

Mechanical Design (Duchamp)
c.1956–7
Dessin pour un mécanique (Duchamp)
Black felt-tip pen on paper
50 x 31.5 cm
Museum Tinguely, Basel

Miracle Machine, Méta-Kandinsky I
1956
Wundermaschine, Méta-Kandinsky I
Panel with painted metal elements,
wooden wheels, metal rods, rubber
belt, electric motor
39.8 x 103.2 x 33 cm
Museum Tinguely, Basel

Black and White Relief Méta-
Mécanique 1957
Relief Méta-mécanique blanc et noir
Black painted iron, white masonite,
electric motor
125 x 185.5 cm
Moderna Museet, Stockholm.
Donation 1961 from the artist

Drawing created by Méta-matic
No.8 (for Eva Aeppli) 3 July 1959
Coloured felt-tip pen on card
20.5 x 15.5 cm
Museum Tinguely, Basel

Drawing created by Méta-matic
No.8 1959
Coloured felt-tip pen on card
21 x 15 cm
Museum Tinguely, Basel

Drawing created by Méta-matic
No.10 1959
Black felt-tip pen on red paper
44 x 38.8 cm
Museum Tinguely, Basel

Drawing created by Méta-matic
No.11 by Hansjörg Stoecklin
18 May 1959
Coloured felt-tip pen on paper
46 x 40 cm
Museum Tinguely, Basel

Drawing created by Méta-matic
No.12 by J. Kosics 1959
Coloured felt-tip pen on paper
46 x 38.8 cm
Museum Tinguely, Basel

Drawing made at the ICA by
Méta-matic No.10/12 1959
Felt-tip pen on paper
1000 x 27 cm
Museum Tinguely, Basel

Méta-matic No.7 1959
Painted metal, wire, steel, rubber
belts, electric motor and paper
55.5 x 94.5 x 50 cm
Private Collection, courtesy Galerie
Natalie Seroussi, Paris

Méta-matic No.17 1959
Painted iron, wood, paper
330 x 172 x 193 cm
Moderna Museet, Stockholm.
Donation 1965 from the Friends
of Moderna Museet

Sketch for Méta-matic No.17 with
Photograph 1959
Marker pen on paper with black
and white photograph
30 x 42.5 cm
Museum Tinguely, Basel

Fragment from *Homage to New York*
(suicide carriage) 1960
Painted metal, fabric, tape, wood,
and rubber tires
203.7 x 75.1 x 223.2 cm
The Museum of Modern Art,
New York. Gift of the artist 1968

Hommage à Hoffnung 1960
Pencil on paper
37.5 x 37.5 cm
Collection of Cary Bluhm

Homage to New York 1960
Ink on paper
59 x 9.5 cm
Museum Tinguely, Basel

Fragment from *Homage to New York* (wheels) 1960
Metal, rubber and wire
42.2 x 54.6 x 41 cm
Private Collection, USA

Méta-matic Drawing from 'Homage to New York' 1960
Black ink on paper
30 x 39 cm
Museum Tinguely, Basel

Fragment from *Homage to New York* (fan) 1960
Metal electric fan
45 x 33 x 26.6 cm
Klüver/Martin Archive

Fragment from *Homage to New York* (piano leg) 1960
Painted wood
35.5 x 21 x 5.7 cm
Collection of Cary Bluhm

Vive la Liberté 1960
Scrap metal, wire, rubber, wood, electric motor
43 x 83 x 42 cm
Museum Tinguely, Basel

Méta-matic Drawing by Eva de Buren 1967
Red felt-tip pen on paper
29.8 x 21.3 cm
Museum Tinguely, Basel

Méta-matic Zeichnung by Miriam Tinguely undated
Felt-tip pen on paper
21 x 27 cm
Museum Tinguely, Basel

Robert Breer

Homage to Jean Tinguely's 'Homage to New York' 1960
16mm film, black and white, optical sound
Duration: 9 minutes 20 seconds
gb agency, Paris

D. A. Pennebaker

Breaking it up at the Museum 1960
Film, black and white, sound
Duration: 8 minutes
Pennebaker Hegedus Films

Michael Landy

H2NY Addressograph Falls Over 2006
Correction fluid on paper
42 x 30 cm
Zabludowicz Collection

H2NY Addressograph Machine Lays Dying 2006
Correction fluid on paper
30 x 42 cm
Zabludowicz Collection

H2NY Alien Death 2006
Correction fluid on paper
21 x 30 cm
Courtesy Joanna Thornberry

H2NY Blazing Sculpture 'Watered Down', The Stars and Stripes 2006
Oil stick on paper
122 x 153 cm
Private Collection

H2NY Fantasy Machine 2006
Correction fluid on paper
29.8 x 21 cm
Courtesy Linda and Andrew Robb, Perth, Australia

H2NY Gizmo Runs Wild Reflecting our Era 2006
Correction fluid on paper
21 x 29.8 cm
Jason Dungan, London

H2NY Inorganic Ending 2006
Correction fluid on paper
30 x 21 cm
Courtesy Thomas Dane Gallery, London

H2NY Large Méta-matic 2006
Correction fluid on paper
42 x 30 cm
Zabludowicz Collection

H2NY Machine Comedy with Ironic Ending 2006
Correction fluid on paper
29.8 x 42 cm
Collection Adam Gahlin and Tieu Pham

140

H2NY Metallic Suicide 2006
Glue and gouache on paper
152 x 122 cm
Lodeveans Collection, London

*H2NY Mr Tinguely makes Fools
of Machines* 2006
Glue and gouache on paper
101.6 x 66.7 cm
Courtesy of Alexander and Bonin
Gallery, New York

H2NY Picture-making Machine II
2006
Oil stick on paper
152 x 122 cm
Lodeveans Collection, London

*H2NY Self-constructing,
Self-destroying* 2006
Oil stick on paper
152.5 x 122 cm
Jeremy Lewison Ltd

*H2NY Self-Constructing, Self-
destroying Tinguely Machine,
Museum of Modern Art, 17 March
1960* 2006
Charcoal on paper
150 x 227 cm
Tate. Purchased 2007

*H2NY Self-destroying Sculpture
Garden* 2006
70 x 81 cm
Ink on paper
Collection of Oliver Barker and
Robert Norman

*H2NY The Audience Gave a Rousing
Cheer for the Dying Monster* 2006
Correction fluid on paper
30 x 42 cm
Zabludowicz Collection

H2NY The Crowd 2006
Correction fluid on paper
42 x 30 cm
Zabludowicz Collection

H2NY The Fire 2006
Correction fluid on paper
30 x 42 cm
Zabludowicz Collection

*H2NY The Notes Played Wistfully
Out of Tune* 2006
Correction fluid on paper
59.3 x 83.9 cm
Courtesy Thomas Dane Gallery,
London

*H2NY The Tinguely Machine Beats
Itself into a Fiery Frenzy* 2006
Correction fluid on paper
30 x 42 cm
Private Collection, Courtesy Karsten
Schubert, London

*H2NY The Tinguely Machine,
The Village Voice* 2006
Oil stick on paper
59.2 x 84 cm
Private Collection, London

H2NY Three Piano Notes 2006
Correction fluid on paper
59.8 x 84 cm
Arts Council Collection, Southbank
Centre, London

*H2NY Tinguely's Machine Lies in
Ruins* 2006
Correction fluid on paper
30 x 42 cm
Zabludowicz Collection

H2NY Tinguely Tinkers 2006
Correction fluid on paper
21 x 29.8 cm
Collection Simon Marlow and
Francesca Urquhart

H2NY Auto-Destructive Edifice 2007
Oil stick on paper
244 x 153 cm
Collection Defares, Amsterdam

*H2NY An Unbeautiful Joke with
No Punch Line* 2007
Correction fluid on paper
83.9 x 59.3 cm
Private Collection, London

H2NY Futile Ends 2007
Correction fluid on paper
83.9 x 59.3 cm
Private Collection

H2NY Homage to New York 2007
Oil stick on paper
153 x 244 cm
Courtesy Gordon Watson, London

*H2NY MoMA Sculpture Garden,
17th March 1960* 2007
Ink on paper
100 x 170 cm
Private Collection

H2NY Skeleton of the Dump 2007
Oil stick on paper
123 x 153 cm
Galerie Nathalie Obadia, Paris

H2NY Theatre of Junk 2007
Correction fluid on paper
59.3 x 83.9 cm
Mark Hix, London

*H2NY Their Time Rubs Out,
They Destroy Themselves* 2007
Correction fluid on paper
83.9 x 59.3 cm
Mark Hix, London

*H2NY Tinguely's Self-destroying
Sculpture Drowns Itself in Maillol's,
'The River'* 2007
Oil stick on paper
122 x 304 cm
Luc Bellier, Paris

H2NY My Head on his Shoulders
2007
Digital photograph
122 x 80 cm
Courtesy Thomas Dane Gallery, London

H2NY 2009
Video, colour, sound
Duration 27 minutes
The Channel 4 BRITDOC Foundation

Sponsors and Donors

Adam Mickiewicz Institute
The Art Fund
Arts and Business
Arts Council England
BT
Business in the Arts: North West
DLA Piper
John Entwistle
Esmée Fairbairn Foundation
European Regional Development Fund
Horace W Goldsmith Foundation
The Granada Foundation
KPMG Foundation
Liverpool City Council
Manchester Airport Group
Margrit Hahnloser
North West Business Leadership Team
North West Regional Development Agency
Peter Cruddas Foundation
PH Holt Foundation
Pro Helvetia, Swiss Arts Council
Tate Liverpool Members
Tate Members
Unilever UK

Corporate Members

Andrew Collinge Ltd
Alder Hey Imagine Appeal, supported by Assura Group
Arup
Bank of Scotland Corporate
Barlows Plc
Beetham Organisation
Betafence Ltd
Brabners Chaffe Street LLP
British Waterways
Bruntwood
Cheetham Bell JWT
Deutsche Bank Private Wealth Management
Downtown Liverpool in Business
Dr Foster Ltd
Grant Thornton
Grosvenor
Individual Restaurant Company
KPMG
Lime Pictures
Midas Capital Partners Ltd
Novartis Vaccines & Diagnostics Ltd
Royal Bank of Scotland
Silverbeck Rymer
Taylor Young Ltd
Trowers & Hamlins

Corporate Partners

Accenture (UK) Ltd
David M Robinson (Jewellery) Ltd
DLA Piper
DWF
Ethel Austin Property Group
Hill Dickinson
HSBC Bank Plc
Laureate Online Education
Liverpool Hope University
Liverpool John Moores University
The University of Liverpool
Unilever UK

Patrons

Ann Alexander
Diana Barbour
David Bell
Jo Bloxham
Tom Bloxham MBE
Peter Bullivant
Jim Davies
Olwen McLaughlin
Barry Owen

142

Jean Tinguely
Fragment from *Homage to New York* (klaxon), 1960

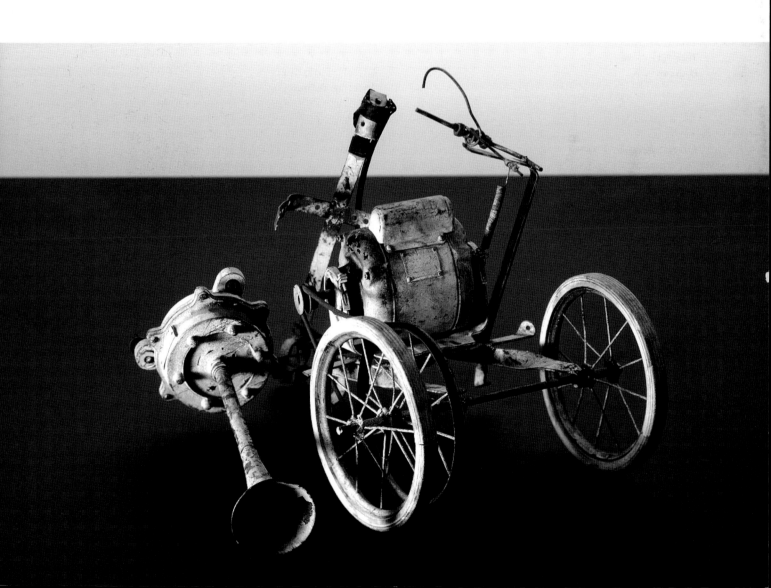

First published 2009 by order of the Tate Trustees
by Tate Liverpool
Albert Dock, Liverpool L3 4BB
in association with
Tate Publishing, a division of Tate Enterprises Ltd,
Millbank, London SW1P 4RG
www.tate.org.uk/publishing

on the occasion of the exhibition
Joyous Machines: Michael Landy and Jean Tinguely
at Tate Liverpool
2 October 2009 until 10 January 2010
curated by Michael Landy and Laurence Sillars

The exhibition is supported by Pro Helvetia, Swiss Arts Council
Additional support provided by Paul and Margrit Hahnloser-Ingold

British Library Cataloguing in Publication Data
A catalogue record for this book is available from the British Library

ISBN 978-1-85437-919-1

Designed by Herman Lelie and Stefania Bonelli
Printed by Graphicom, Italy

Cover: Michael Landy, *H2NY Machine Created to Destroy Tinguely Museum*, 2009
Frontispiece: Michael Landy, *H2NY My Head on His Shoulders*, 2007
(Original photo by Hansjörg Stoecklin of Jean Tinguely in front of
Homage to New York, 1960) © Hansjörg Stoecklin and Michael Landy